To Dr. Bennett Smith
J.
gle.

Ed Steele
2:19:1

God's
Creation
Story

A Scriptural and Scientific
Study of the Creation

Ed Steele

ISBN: 1-4392-3066-8
ISBN-13: 9781439230664

Visit www.booksurge.com to order additional copies.

DEDICATION

This book is lovingly dedicated
to my precious and lovely wife,

Barbara.

She is such a wonderful
Mother and Grandmother.

She thought she was marrying
an Aero-Space Engineer.
But, when God called me into the ministry,
she also answered the call and
became a faithful Pastor's wife
and partner in the ministry.

She has been my best friend and soul mate.
I love her very much and
thank God for her every day!

TABLE OF CONTENTS

FOREWARD

*"Who knoweth whether thou art come to
the kingdom for such a time as this?"* (Esther 4:14).

This was the question that Mordecai asked Queen Esther. It surely caused her to consider her position in the kingdom and how it had come to be.

The parents of Esther had both died and she had been raised by her cousin Mordecai. Queen Vashti had been the wife of King Ahasuerus but had been dethroned because she refused to dance at his drunken party. The King had sent forth a decree for all the fair virgins to come and compete to be his new Queen. Esther was chosen, but no one knew that she was a Jew. Haman was promoted by the King to be over all the princes of his kingdom. He had a hatred for all Jews, but his special hatred was directed toward Mordecai. He made a request of the King that all the Jews be killed, and he even built a scaffold specifically to hang Mordecai. The King approved the request and Mordecai knew that all the Jews were in danger. He put on sackcloth and ashes and went into the midst of the city and began to cry out with a loud and bitter cry.

When Esther was told about Mordecai's actions, she sent forth a messenger to determine the cause of his grief. Mordecai revealed the decree and urged her to go before her husband on the behalf of her people. She reminded him that if she went before the King unsolicited, that she would be in danger of being killed. It was at that point that Mordecai asked her the probing question.

She realized that she would not be Queen had her parents not died. If Mordecai had not taken care of her, she would not be in this position. If Vashti had not refused to comply with the King's request, he would not have needed another Queen. She had been chosen from a large group of other young virgins who were also worthy of being chosen. Considering all of these things, she began to see the sovereign hand of God that had brought all these things to pass, God knowing that His people would be in danger and someone needed to be there to save them. She was there "For such a time as this."

Esther went before the King knowing the danger but trusting that the same God who put her there would also deliver her. Because of her intervention, her people were delivered and Haman was hanged on the very scaffold that he had built for Mordecai.

It is important for each of us to look back over the events and circumstances of our lives to see that the sovereignty of God has also brought us to where we are today to serve His purpose according to His will. This is certainly true for me.

When I was in high school, my Mother's oldest brother (Dorrance Anderson) was an Electrical Engineer for NASA at Marshall Space Flight Center in Huntsville, Alabama. He was one of my heroes and I wanted to follow in his steps. He knew that I was not financially able to go to an engineering school, so he advised me to go to a local college and major in mathematics and physics - a degree that would prepare me to do the work of an engineer.

As I enrolled in college, I looked at the catalog and saw the classes offered in electronics and was very excited. But, during my time at the school those classes were never taught. Instead, I took subjects dealing with the physical sciences of the laws of motion, forces and moments. I felt disappointed in not being able to fulfill my dream of working in the field of electronics. God had something else in mind for me, although I did not realize it at the time.

When I went to work at the Marshall Space Flight Center in Huntsville, I was assigned to work in the area of aerodynamics and trajectories. There were many outstanding engineers, but I was assigned to work under the leadership of Mike Naumcheff. Mike was one of the engineers who designed predicted trajectories for each mission. He was one of the best engineers with whom I ever worked. Mike took me under his wings and trained me. I would later work at the Manned Spacecraft Center (now Johnson Space Center) in Houston, Texas, and the Michoud Operations in New Orleans, Louisiana, where I continued to use the science and engineering he had taught me. I could never have found a better person to have as a mentor! Some would call it luck, but I know that God designed it all!

When I surrendered to the ministry in July, 1969, our church had just called a new pastor, Bro. Bob Bullock. He began teaching a Bible study on creation, and from him I learned what the Bible really teaches on the subject. He revealed from the Bible that the earth could be very old, but the current creation on earth was relatively new. This was something I had never heard before! I will always be grateful for the influence this man of God had on my life!

I treasure the years that I spent working for NASA. I also feel blessed to have been taught by Bro. Bullock and to have the privilege of reading the works of many great Christian writers who also expounded on the subject of creation. My life experiences are not an accident. God has me here for such a time as this!

It is my desire to use this book to present the truth about creation from a scientific and scriptural viewpoint, understanding that true science can never conflict with an accurate interpretation of Scripture. God has blessed me with many wonderful experiences that give me a unique perspective of what He has done. I pray that God will use this book about "God's Creation Story" to bless each reader as He has blessed me.

PREFACE

The gospel of our Lord Jesus Christ is the primary message that must be proclaimed with all the power given us by the Holy Spirit (Acts 1:8). That was the attitude of the Apostle Paul: *"For I delivered unto you first of all that which I also received, how that Christ died for our sins according to the scriptures; And that he was buried, and that he rose again the third day according to the scriptures"* (1 Corinthians 15:3, 4).

All studies from Scripture are important (such as creation), but the gospel that leads lost souls to Jesus for salvation must be our first priority! Therefore, it is absolutely imperative that we never do or say anything that would hinder anyone from believing the message of the gospel of our Lord Jesus Christ.

It is possible that some people who know us will not accept our message if our lives are not consistent with what we preach. The Apostle Paul reminded the church at Thessalonica that he had not only preached to them, but had also lived among them in a godly manner. *"For our gospel came not unto you in word only, but also in power, and in the Holy Ghost, and in much assurance; as ye know what manner of men we were among you for your sake"* (1 Thessalonians 1:5).

The Thessalonians became believers because his life had not distracted from his message. *"Ye are witnesses, and God also, how holily and justly and unblameably we behaved ourselves among you that believe"* (1 Thessalonians 2:10). Never allow the power of the gospel to be nullified by what people see in your life!

It is also possible that what we teach on other subjects may be so filled with error that people will doubt the truth of the gospel when we try to share it with them. They will be prone to believe that if we are wrong in one area then they will doubt us in other areas as well. Creation is one subject that has caused many to reject everything else that is taught in the Bible. This is because they really do not know what the Bible says about creation.

Many Christians have assumed and taught that all creation began just a few thousand years ago. The media and educational institutions seem to assume this is a universal view by all creationists. That is far from the truth! Many dedicated Bible scholars believe that the Bible teaches the possibility of the universe and solar system being very old. They believe that a few thousand years ago the earth was a dead planet without life. The six days work made the earth an inhabitable planet again. God then created new life (including Adam and Eve) to live on the newly restored earth. Regrettably, many are not even aware of this theory.

Scientific and geological discoveries have led many to believe that the earth is very old. Fossil remains and rock formations reveal that earth has gone through many catastrophic upheavals at some time in the past. When people who are aware of the geological ages of the earth are told emphatically that the Bible teaches it is just a few thousand years old, they are tempted to doubt the truthfulness of the Bible. This leads to the mistaken belief that there are errors in the Bible, and they do not give proper consideration to the gospel of Jesus Christ.

This book will provide many reasons to believe that the original creation of heaven and earth is recorded in Genesis 1:1. Heaven refers to everything that is above us and earth is the planet beneath us. I believe that God created many creatures to live on the original earth through eons of time. Fossils have been found in successive levels of sedimentary rock all over the earth. Many of these fossils are of animals which are extinct. For example, dinosaurs suddenly came into existence, and then just as quickly, millions of years later they disappeared. Their existence was not an accident, but an act of God's creative power. No life could have ever existed on earth without God's creative power! I believe He is likely the reason that many species became extinct as well.

There came a time when the earth became uninhabitable. Genesis 1:2 describes the uninhabitable state of the earth. God then used the six days work to restore the earth to the home we enjoy today. Our earth is the same planet that was originally created. It makes sense then that earth bears the signs of many catastrophic and cataclysmic events that happened to it a very long time ago. These events ultimately resulted in it becoming without form and void. The earth also reveals evidence of plants and animals that once existed here long ago, indicating that we were not among the first ones to inhabit the earth.

The Bible is God's revelation to mankind. Primarily, it reveals what God has done on earth since the creation of Adam and Eve to provide salvation for fallen man and how man can receive that salvation. However, the Genesis account of creation does give us assurance that God is the Creator of all things and we are totally dependent on Him. While most of the Bible deals with His work on the six days and thereafter, it does give a glimpse back to some things that happened prior to that time. This book will seek to open up the window to that earlier time to help you understand that we are a fairly young creation that is living on a very old planet.

When reasonable scientists realize what the Bible really teaches, they understand that their discoveries are consistent with biblical teachings. Far too many Christians feel threatened when scientists teach about an old earth because they don't understand that any true discovery that is made can only reveal what God has done. Our eternal God has always been here and anything discovered in earth or space only reveals the glory of His presence and power!

I realize that many Bible believers will refuse to believe the earth is old because they accept by faith that it is very young. They prefer to accept by faith that the dinosaurs only lived a few thousand years ago and disregard all evidence to the contrary. It is admirable to have faith, but there is no virtue in having faith in something that is not true!

It is my desire to present scriptural and scientific evidence that we are a young creation living on an old earth. Hopefully, the Christian will begin to glorify God in all legitimate scientific discoveries, and scientists will be led to God by the truth of the Scriptures. More importantly, it is my prayer that many young people who believe in creation will study this book and not be led astray by those things they are taught in the future. Scripture presents God as the Creator of all things and scientific discoveries only reveal what He did. Therefore, Christian and scientist alike should glorify God for what is revealed in "God's Creation Story".

Chapter 1
IN THE BEGINNING

The only eyewitness to what happened in the beginning was God Himself. Men have always searched for answers to two important questions. First, how did the creation of the solar system and all that is found in the universe become a reality? Second, how did living creatures come to be on the earth? There are numerous views concerning answers to these very important questions.

Scientific discoveries by geologists, archaeologists, anthropologists, astronomers, etc., have led some to reach their conclusions. Their conclusions, however, are based only on speculations or theories. The acts of creation and life cannot be duplicated in a laboratory! The works of God in the beginning were singular events that cannot be copied by any effort of man. Scientists can only use the things that are a part of God's creation. God was able to make a visible creation out of things that cannot be seen.

"Through faith we understand that the worlds were framed by the word of God, so that things which are seen were not made of things which do appear"

(Hebrews 11:3).

There are numerous verses about creation found in Scripture that dedicated and honest Bible students interpret in various ways. There can be no doubt that the Bible declares that God did create all things, but exactly when and how the creation occurred can be a matter of disagreement. There are some things on which devoted Bible students should agree. The Bible is very clear in declaring that it is the inspired, infallible and inerrant Word of God. The gospel message that Jesus died on a rugged cross, arose from a borrowed tomb, and ascended to sit on His Father's right hand to be our great High Priest is very clearly presented in the Bible. The sufficiency and efficiency of the precious blood of Jesus Christ in providing redemption for sinful man is a biblical truth that cannot be denied. There can be no doubt that the Bible presents Jesus Christ as the only Savior for man and that man can only be saved when he repents of his sins and places his faith in Jesus. These and many more doctrines can be believed with certainty, but the how and when of creation are not as certain.

True science and the Bible will always agree. However, not everything that is taught as science is necessarily true! The Apostle Paul warned Timothy about science (or knowledge) that was not based on truth: *"O Timothy, keep that which is committed to thy trust, avoiding profane and vain babblings, and oppositions of science falsely so called"* (1 Timothy 6:20).

It is also true that not every interpretation that an individual has of Scripture is necessarily accurate either! The truthfulness of the Bible is never to be judged by what is taught by science. The accuracy of scientific teachings can be verified when it agrees with what is presented in the Bible. The Bible is the only standard to which all other theories and beliefs should be compared!

Some scientists often look upon the Christian with disdain because he accepts the biblical account of creation by faith. The truth is that those scientists accept their theories by faith as well! After many years of searching and spending billions of dollars, evolutionists have been unable to find appropriate proof of evolution or any of their other theories as to how the solar system came into existence. Everyone sees the beginning by faith!

The object of one's faith makes a great difference when he looks back on what happened in the beginning. When the believer looks back, all he sees is God. The Bible opens with the statement, *"In the beginning God"* (Genesis 1:1a). When some others look back, they only see a spinning mass, but they have no idea from where the mass came.

When one believes in the eternal God Who is the Creator of us all and in the veracity (the complete truth) of Holy Scripture, the fact of the creation of all things and all living creatures should be easily accepted. But there are not enough verses giving details about creation for anyone to be adamant about the how and when. We have to take all the verses that are available and establish a theory that is consistent with Who God is and what His Word teaches. If the theory is accurate, it will agree with true scientific discoveries.

Therefore, I believe there are three things that should be considered in determining whether a theory of the beginning has any validity:

1. Is God presented as the Creator of all things?

2. Is the biblical account of creation given proper consideration?

3. Is it consistent with proven scientific knowledge?

When the answer is in the affirmative for all three questions the theory should at least be given consideration. When one of the answers is negative, the theory has failed the test for validity.

The five most popular theories about the origin of the solar system will be evaluated based on these considerations. The solar system includes the sun, all its planets, the moons of the various planets, and all life that is on earth. It should be readily apparent that some who agree on a certain theory could differ somewhat on some of the particulars of that theory, but the basic views will be consistent. Of course the One who created the solar system is also the One who created the rest of the vast universe, but most theories limit themselves as to how the solar system came into being.

<u>Natural Phenomena Produced Everything By Chance</u>

The vast majority of the body of scientists and educators present their belief that the creation happened by chance from natural causes. Yet, there have been many views about what really happened. Some believe that a "Big Bang" brought the universe into existence. More on this theory about the beginning of the universe will be discussed in a later chapter. For now, the theories concerning the creation of the solar system will be presented.

In 1796, Marquis Pierre Simon de LaPlace came up with the Nebular Theory.[1] He proposed that a large gaseous cloud (or nebula) was spinning and it began to contract as it cooled.

As it became smaller, it spun faster and faster with the individual planets being thrown off into their respective orbits. The part left in the center became the sun. In like manner, the planets were spinning and their moons were thrown off into orbits as well. Mr. LaPlace would have trouble explaining why individual moons around Jupiter are going in opposite directions!

In 1905, geologist T. C. Chamberlin and astronomer F. R. Maulton presented the Planetary Hypothesis whereby they proposed that a giant star with a large gravitational pull passed close to the sun pulling material away that would become planets[2].

Numerous other theories have been advanced through the years trying to explain how the solar system came into being. No effort has been fully accepted by all scientists. It should be noted that scientists have been unable to come up with a valid theory for the beginning of just the solar system much less the vast universe of stars and galaxies!

Even more difficult has been the effort to explain the origination of all living creatures on earth. Since Charles Darwin's *"Origin Of The Species"* was written in 1859, most who believe that all things exist by chance hold to the belief that all species exist because of evolution. This is in spite of the fact that no evidence has ever been found proving that any species has come from another one. Also, no creature has ever been found that was in the process of evolving into another species. It will remain Darwin's *theory* because there is no proof to validate it. It fails the test!

These theories about the beginning of the solar system must be rejected because none of them can be proven using the known laws of physical science and thermodynamics as will be revealed in a later chapter. They all fail the test of scientific knowledge, yet they are being taught in schools and scientific circles as though they were fact. In addition, their theory that man evolved from a lower life form must be rejected because it is against the Word of God that clearly teaches that all mankind are descendants of Adam and Eve who were created by God.

The possibility that there is a God who brought everything into being is never given consideration by those who believe that natural causes did it all. Many of them even deny that there is a God! Since they give God no credit, then His Word is ignored and the biblical account of creation is no more than a fable to them.

Therefore, those who propose the theories that natural phenomena produced everything by chance have failed on all three of the questions for determining validity! Their theories will never be fact!

Natural Phenomena Produced Under Providential Direction (Theistic Evolution)

Many of the theories taught by the former group are also espoused by the Theistic evolution group as well. They have been influenced by what is taught and presented in the secular world about how the solar system, stars, etc., all came about from an explosion or from gases. Since they believe that the natural world came about by chance, then it is easy for them to also believe that all living creatures exist by chance as well. Thus, the evolution of man from a lower life form is accepted.

While this group holds many of the theories of those who deny God's part in creation, they still want to hold on to their belief in God. How can they harmonize the belief that all things happened naturally, yet still believe there is a God? They form the theory that God was in control and brought about the condition of gases becoming a solar system and man evolving. Thus, they accept the theories of the scientific world, but still trust in God and try to give Him credit for being the Creator.

They accept God as Creator so they pass the first proposed question for validity. However, they fail the second question since they totally ignore the teaching of God's Word and its account of instant creation. Since they hold to the same false scientific beliefs as the former group, they fail the third question as well. Therefore, their theory of creation coming about by natural means under the providential power of God must be rejected.

<u>Six Long Time Periods Used in Creation (Day Period Theory)</u>

There are some who hold to the theory that the six days of creation mentioned in the first chapter of Genesis were really six long periods of time. This belief may result from what they see as scientific evidence proving that the earth is much older than the chronological time recorded from the beginning of the Bible until now. They believe in God and in the accuracy of Holy Scripture so their interpretation provides enough time for the earth to be much older than a few thousand years. It is true that sometimes the use of the word 'day' in Scripture does mean something different than a 24 hour period of time: *"But, beloved, be not ignorant of this one thing, that one day is with the Lord as a thousand years, and a thousand years as one day"* (2 Peter 3:8).

According to this theory, the first day when light was given to the earth was a long period of time. The second day of waters being divided was also lengthy. On the third day dry land was made to appear and it would take a long period of time for all the trees and grass to grow. Therefore, the earth would be ready for all the creatures that would be created on the fifth and sixth days. In like manner, the creatures that were created at the beginning of the fifth day could have been created a long time before those created at the end of the day. This would leave a fossil record that some creatures appeared on earth at different times. This is the basic logic that is used to justify believing in day periods. There is a problem, however, since science has revealed that fossil records were left on earth from the earliest times and not after four long periods of time.

At the conclusion of each of the six days, the statement was made that it was the *"evening and morning"* of that particular day (Genesis 1:5, 8, 13, 19, 23, 31). God rested on the seventh day from all His work and sanctified it: *"And on the seventh day God ended his work which he had made; and he rested on the seventh day from all his work which he had made. And God blessed the seventh day, and sanctified it: because that in it he had rested from all his work which God created and made"* (Genesis 2:2, 3). The Sabbath was established for man to work six days and then rest the seventh, as God had done in His work of creation: *"For in six days the LORD made heaven and earth, the sea, and all that in them is, and rested the seventh day: wherefore the LORD blessed the sabbath day, and hallowed it"* (Exodus 20:11). A similar verse is also found in Exodus 31:17. The adherents of the day period theory believe that God gave a record of six days just to leave us an example of how we should work six days and rest the seventh. It seems like He could have left us an example another way and it is best to accept the biblical record as a literal six days.

One other thing that casts doubt about the day period theory that the work on each day took a long period of time is that the Bible states creation came about by a divine fiat. God simply said, "Let it be". The following verses reveal that the work of creation occurred simply by the spoken word of God:

> *"By the word of the LORD were the heavens made; and all the host of them by the breath of his mouth. He gathereth the waters of the sea together as an heap: he layeth up the depth in storehouses. Let all the earth fear the LORD: let all the inhabitants of the world stand in awe*

of him.   For he spake, and it was done; he commanded, and it stood fast" (Psalm 33:6-9)

"Through faith we understand that the worlds were framed by the word of God, so that things which are seen were not made of things which do appear" (Hebrews 11:3)

There is no reason (biblical or otherwise) to believe that the creative events God spoke into place would require some period of time to be manifested after He spoke.

The proponents of the day period theory believe that the earth is older than just a few thousand years. They believe very firmly that God is the Creator of the universe and the giver of life to every living thing. They also believe in the Bible, but I do not agree with their interpretation of the work done in the six days as recorded in Genesis 1.

When compared to the three questions for validity they do very well. However, the belief that each "day" was a long period of time surely changes how this group views the how and when of the beginning. It could also affect how much time they believe has elapsed since the creation of Adam and Eve. The historical record of Adam's race on earth seems to reveal that we have only been here a few thousand years. It was just a few thousand years ago that men were first suddenly found on earth leaving a written history as they built cities, pyramids, etc.   Indeed, one can argue that man has not evolved from that first introduction, but rather devolved!

I appreciate the ones who hold this theory much more than those who have the beliefs described by the first two theories. They give God all the credit and glory and they do believe His Word. They just understand it differently than I do.

Six Days of Creative Work (Young Earth Theory)

The adherents of this theory believe that heaven and earth were both created in the six days that are described in Genesis 1. They believe that everything that has been created was created in those six days. Thus, they believe that the earth, the solar system and the entire universe are only a few thousand years old. While they agree that scientific discoveries make the earth to appear very old, they believe it was either created with an "apparent age" or the effects of Noah's flood (the Deluge) cause it to have the appearance of being very old. Those who hold to this theory will be referred to as Young Earth Creationists (YECs).

These beliefs were presented in the book *"The Genesis Flood"* written by John C. Whitcomb and Henry M. Morris in 1961. Henry Morris later started the "Institute for Creation Research" in El Cajon, California, where the young Earth theory was taught with great acceptance in the Christian community. It now has a branch in Texas. Many other organizations have grown out of the teachings from this first book.

Ken Ham instituted "Answers In Genesis". His organization has written many books and produced many videos espousing this theory as though it was fact. I have been receiving his bi-monthly newsletter for several years. He opened a museum near Cincinnati, Ohio, in 2007, that he reports cost $27,000,000.00. This money came from donations and the profit from the sales of his books and videos.

Kent Hovind started "Creation Science Evangelism" in 1989. Using this organization, he was widely used as a speaker at churches and colleges presenting the young earth theory. He started the Dinosaur Adventure Land theme park in Pensacola, Florida, in 2001. Many youth groups from churches throughout the southeastern part of the United States have visited the park where they have been taught about humans co-existing with dinosaurs less than 6,000 years ago. His organization produced many videos and books depicting the belief of a young earth.

When calculating the dates given in the Bible using the ages of the various patriarchs, the history of Adam's race on earth would only be about 6,000 years old. Since they believe that Adam was created just five days after heaven and earth, they believe that all the rest of creation is only 6,000 years old as well. They date the creation to 4004 b. c. There are many YECs, however, who believe that the Earth is several thousand years older.

In Genesis 5, the genealogy of ten generations before the flood from Adam to Noah is given with the next generation having three prominent sons – Ham, Shem, and Japheth. In Genesis 11, the genealogy of ten generations from Shem to Terah after the flood is given with the next generation also having three prominent sons – Abram, Nahor, and Haran. The chronology of the time given in Genesis 11 from Shem to Terah only gives a span of about 500 years. It was in that period when the languages were changed at the tower of Babel resulting in the various races being separated from one another (Genesis 11:1-9). Yet, in Abram's day many civilizations and empires had already been established. This causes many YECs to believe that the time from Noah to Abram was in fact much longer than 500 years, so they do not hold to the 4004 b. c. date of creation.

Henry Morris and John Whitcomb taught that the purpose of Genesis 11 was not to give an account of age, so they believed it represented a time much greater than 500 years.

If the strict-chronology interpretation of Genesis 11 is correct, *all* the postdiluvian patriarchs, including Noah, would still have been living when Abram was fifty years old; *three* of those who were born before the earth was divided (Shem, Shelah, and Eber) would have actually outlived Abram, but would have lived for two years after Jacob arrived in Mesopotamia to work for Laban!

As we follow Abram in his wanderings, from Ur of the Chaldees to the land of Canaan, filled to overflowing with "the Kenite, and the Kenizzite, the Amorite, and the Canaanite, and Girgashite, and the Jebusite" (Genesis 15:19-21); and then follow him down into the land of Egypt with its Pharoah and its princes (12:15); and then see him going to Lot's rescue in the vicinity of Damascus after Lot and other captives from the five cities of the Plain had been deported by the kings of Shinar, Ellaser, Elam, and Goiim (14:1-16); and then see him being met by a priest-king of Salem (14:18); and later see him coming into contact with a Philistine king (20:2) and Hittite landowners (23:2-20), we cannot help but feel that the judgment of God upon the Tower of Babel must have occurred many centuries before the time of Abram.[3]

Neither Ham nor Hovind agree with this interpretation of Genesis 11. They both adhere to the date of creation being in 4004 b. c. and teach such in their books and videos. The scriptural references given by Morris seem adequate to prove that the period from the flood to the call of Abram was most likely several thousand years long as he believed.

While most YECs present their young earth beliefs as facts rather than theories, Morris seemed to teach what he considered 'possibilities' in his explanations. This is revealed in the following quote when he discussed the possibility of how canyons were formed on the ocean floor as a result of Noah's flood (the Deluge).

> It would seem, on the other hand, that Deluge conditions, as inferred from the Scriptural record, could give a reasonable explanation for their origin. -- It may well have been that the turbidity currents entering the canyons may have deepened and extended them still further, a process which has continued on a smaller scale throughout the centuries since.[4]

His use of 'it would seem', 'could give', 'may well have' and 'may have deepened' shows that he only presented them as possibilities.

The YECs believe that the creation described in the first two verses of Genesis 1 happened on the first day of the six days work. The Bible is the best interpreter of itself. We cannot believe something because it helps to validate our other beliefs. The scriptures that detail the work of days two through six all begin with the same three words, *"And God said"* (Genesis 1:6, 9, 14, 20, 24). Now if those words were used consistently for those days, how would you expect the description of the work done on day one to begin? It is in verse 3 that we find the words: *"And God said, Let there be light: and there was light"*. If the Bible is allowed to interpret itself then the interpreter will see the description of the first day beginning in Genesis 1:3.

If the first day of the six days work begins in the third verse, then the first two verses that reveal the creation of heaven and earth establishes that they existed before the first day began. The question then becomes, how long were they in existence before the events of verse three? Were they there for fifteen minutes? Were they there for fifteen years? Or, could they have been in existence for fifteen million years? There is no way of knowing how long! We just know they were there before the six days work began.

I do not agree with the scientific proofs used by those who hold to the young earth theory. They agree that the earth has signs of great age, but they credit the flood of Noah's day for most of the damage that has been done to the earth. I have read their writings, watched their videos, and heard Hovind speak at one of his engagements, so I am well aware of the science they teach and verses they use to support their theory. I will present what they teach, and then address what I consider to be their errors in detail in a later chapter.

I totally agree with their belief that man was created just a few thousand years ago, and that all living creatures in our world were created by God's hand at the same time to reproduce after their own kind. As stated earlier, historical records left by our forefathers only confirm what the Bible teaches - man has only been on earth for a relatively short time. However, I do not agree with their interpretation and use of Scripture in trying to prove that the earth is as young as Adam and his descendants upon the earth.

The first question for validity concerned the recognition of God as Creator. They do present God as the one and only Creator. The second question is used to evaluate their use of the biblical account of creation in forming their theory. They do use the biblical account for some of their beliefs, although I disagree with many of their interpretations. I do not believe, however, that their scientific teachings are consistent with proved scientific knowledge. They fail the third test.

From Ruin To Restoration of the Earth (Gap Theory)

A large number of people (including me) have a theory that Genesis 1:1 tells about the original creation of the heaven and the earth. They believe that this was a beautiful creation of perfection. Verse 2 then tells of the earth's condition at a later time when it was in a state of being without form and void with darkness covering it. During the time between these two verses, great judgments came upon the earth. Thus, it has been given the name "The Gap Theory" because of the gap of time that exists between the verses. I prefer to call it the "Ruin To Restoration" theory. Those who hold this belief will be referred to as RTRs.

The condition of the earth as being without form and void is the description of its condition just prior to the six days work. There is no way to know how long it was in that condition or how long it had been since God originally created the heaven and the earth. All we are told in Genesis 1:2 is that the earth was in a state of ruin. The six days work was a time of restoration of the earth to a perfect condition, and God then created fishes, fowls, animals, creeping things and humans to dwell upon that perfect place.

The RTRs believe that the original earth that was created in the beginning according to Genesis 1:1 was a beautiful place and could have been in existence for a very long time. They believe it was once inhabited by many creatures whose deaths have left many fossil records on the earth. It could have been inhabited by dinosaurs and many other creatures that are totally foreign to the world that we live in. Prehistoric man-like creatures could have lived upon that earth as well. A judgment, or a series of judgments, came to earth that resulted in it becoming a dead planet and all the creatures that lived on it were killed.

The earth we live on bears many signs of having gone through cataclysmic events. I agree with the YECs that the flood could have caused some changes. Volcanoes and earthquakes that have occurred since the six days work could also have left their marks on the geological discoveries. However, there are too many signs that reveal judgments from millions of years ago for all the damage to have been done in the last few thousand years. The RTRs believe that planet earth went through many catastrophes and convulsions during the time between the first two verses of the Bible.

I believe there are many biblical reasons to accept the teaching that the six days work was a renovation of the earth and not its original creation. I do not believe this solely because of the discoveries that have been made by scientists. It just so happens that the discoveries that have been made, and may be made in the future, are easily explained when the earth is viewed as having gone through a ruin and restoration.

The work done by God on the first four days restored the earth to a beautiful planet suitable for life. On the next two days, God created all the living things that He wanted to dwell on that earth and commanded them to bring forth after their own kind. We are still enjoying the work of His hands today.

Obviously, if this theory is true then there must have been a reason for the tremendous judgments that would bring the earth to such ruin. The YECs totally deny what has just been described by teaching that Adam committed the first sin and that there was no death or judgment before he sinned. Since Satan tempted them in the form of a serpent, it should be readily apparent that he had already sinned before he tempted Adam and Eve to sin. This will be explained in great detail in a later chapter. The RTRs believe that everything that happened between the first two verses of the Bible were probably results of the judgment that God brought because of Lucifer's sin.

The RTRs give God all the credit for creation, and they use the Bible to best describe what took place on those six days. Thus, they pass the tests of the first two questions. Their belief is consistent with proven scientific knowledge as well. Some of the things that have been discovered on earth occurred before it was without form and void. Other things have happened since that time and the earth bears evidence of it all.

∞

It is my intention to make an honest comparison between the Young Earth Creation theory and the Ruin To Restoration theory, both biblically and scientifically. When members of the media talk about the Christian's view of creation they only present the views of the YECs. As far as they are concerned, if you believe in creation then you have to believe that everything came into existence 6,000 years ago. The same is true in most of our educational institutions as well.

Our young people are told that the Bible teaches that all of creation is very young. When they are told of discoveries showing an old age to the earth, many of them begin to doubt the Bible. These doubts breed other doubts about things taught in the Bible that are definitely true. The devil tells them that if the Bible is wrong about creation then it is also wrong about Jesus and the salvation that He offers. This is of utmost concern!

The YECs believe that the Creator of all is an eternal God Who has always been in existence. Yet, they believe that He did not create anything until just a few thousand years ago. They believe we are living on a very young earth beneath a very young sun, moon and stars. The RTRs believe the earth could be very old and have a long and storied history, because they believe that God could have been doing His work as Creator for a long, long time. Both groups agree we are living in the final days of planet earth: *"And I saw a new heaven and a new earth: for the first heaven and the first earth were passed away"* (Revelation 21:1).

This theory of the ruin and the restoration of the earth is certainly not a new belief. It has been held by fundamental and conservative Christians for hundreds (and maybe thousands) of years. The reader is urged to give prayerful and thoughtful consideration to what will be presented about the creation performed by our great God.

As we look back to the beginning all we should see is the Lord! As we look forward to the ending, we still only see the Lord:

> *"I am Alpha and Omega, the beginning and the ending, saith the Lord, which is, and which was, and which is to come, the Almighty"*
>
> (Revelation 1:8).

May the Lord be all that we see as we continue our study of God's Creation Story!

Chapter 2
BY THE WORD OF GOD

The voice of God is the greatest power known unto man. Men try to build greater and more powerful machines to reach their goals, but all God has to do is speak and His will is accomplished! The greatest effort of man to harness nature has been a failure, but Jesus only had to speak to bring a storm under His control. *"And his disciples came to him, and awoke him, saying, Lord, save us: we perish. And he saith unto them, Why are ye fearful, O ye of little faith? Then he arose, and rebuked the winds and the sea; and there was a great calm. But the men marvelled, saying, What manner of man is this, that even the winds and the sea obey him!"* (Matthew 8:25-27). There have been many great things accomplished by the word of God, but two things stand out – creation and the Bible!

The Bible clearly teaches that all things were created in obedience to the commands of the voice of God: *"By the word of the LORD were the heavens made; and all the host of them by the breath of his mouth. — For he spake, and it was done; he commanded, and it stood fast"* (Psalm 33:6, 9). On each of the six days presented in Genesis 1, the three words *"And God said"* are found as an earth that was without form and void was turned into a beautiful earth prepared to be inhabited by His new creation of man, fowl, fish, and other creatures. Thus, all creation exists as a result of the word of God.

The Bible also claims divine authority for itself. The process of writing the entire canon of holy Scripture involved approximately forty men being used over a period of two thousand years, yet God was the Author of each book. The phrase *"For thus saith the Lord"* is found 413 times. The phrase *"The word of the Lord came"* was used 92 times by various writers. Many other words and phrases could be presented that prove that no writer took responsibility for what he wrote, but acknowledged that God was the true Author speaking and writing through him. Thus, when we state that "Jeremiah wrote", we are in fact saying "God wrote through Jeremiah." The Apostle Paul stated, *"Which things also we speak, not in the words which man's wisdom teacheth, but which the Holy Ghost teacheth; comparing spiritual things with spiritual"* (1 Corinthians 2:13). The Apostle Peter expressed it another way, *"For the prophecy came not in old time by the will of man: but holy men of God spake as they were moved by the Holy Ghost"* (2 Peter 1:21). The Bible is God's self-revelation to man. He does not tell us all that He knows, but all that He wants us to know: *"The secret things belong unto the LORD our God: but those things which are revealed belong unto us and to our children for ever, that we may do all the words of this law"* (Deuteronomy 29:29). It gives us the history of the fall of man and what his sin brought to all creation. Then, it gives us God's plan to send His only begotten Son to redeem all mankind. The Scriptures are very precise when it comes to presenting the truth that salvation and forgiveness of sins are only available through the shedding of innocent blood. The security of the redeemed is also clearly revealed. Anyone desiring to know the reasonable service that God wants from His redeemed can easily receive instruction from the truths found in the Bible. It can truthfully be stated that the Bible is God's love letter to all the descendents of Adam's race. There are many more important things that are true but we are told to accept them by faith because we are not given very many details about them.

All who trust Jesus Christ as their personal Savior will have an eternal home that is called Heaven. The Bible promises it. There are many descriptions found that cause us to believe that it will be a beautiful place and everyone should have a desire to spend eternity in such a place with the Lord. Yet, little detail is given to help us to know very much about it: *"But as it is written, Eye hath not seen, nor ear heard, neither have entered into the heart of man, the things which God hath prepared for them that love him"* (1 Corinthians 2:9). We are told enough to make us know that it is real and that we should be excited about being there one day! Other details must wait.

There is a place called hell that will be the eternal abode of all who do not accept Jesus as Savior. We are told that it is a place of outer darkness, a lake of fire, and a place of eternal torment, but the location of hell and many other details about it are not given to us. Enough is revealed for us to know that it is real and we don't want to go there! We also know enough that we should do everything we can to win others to the Lord so they will be able to discover the beauty of Heaven and not know the torments of hell.

The fact that God is the Creator of all things is another truth that one cannot deny if he believes the Bible. Yet, the details that are given about the "how and when" of creation are very scarce. We are simply told that God is the Creator! To know more about His creation story, it is imperative that we study every text that discusses creation. It is also important that we pay close attention to the words that are used in the various texts and the context in which they are used. Since God is the Author, the words that He gave Moses to use will help us to understand the writings of others when they use the same words. The converse is also true.

The Bible is the best interpreter of itself. A message presented in one text will help to interpret another text where the meaning is not so obvious. For example, many have debated on the little sealed book held in the hand of the One who was sitting on the throne in Revelations 5:1-10. The interpretation can be derived from Jeremiah 32:7-14 where Jeremiah used his right of redemption to purchase his uncle's field. After paying the full price, he subscribed the proof of the purchase in a book that he then sealed. He then charged Baruch to put it away for safe keeping:

> *"Thus saith the LORD of hosts, the God of Israel; Take these evidences, this evidence of the purchase, both which is sealed, and this evidence which is open; and put them in an earthen vessel, that they may continue many days"*
>
> (Jeremiah 32:14).

In a similar manner, Jesus paid the redemption price for all creation as our kinsman Redeemer. This gives us reason to believe that the little book in Revelation was the title deed to all that Jesus had purchased on the cross. It is now in the Father's possession. Therefore, Jesus is the only One who is worthy to take the book and open the seals thereof. He purchased it, so it belongs only to Him!

Since Moses wrote in the Hebrew language, it is important that we know the Hebrew words that he used in presenting the creation story. To adequately understand what God meant by the words used by Moses, it will be helpful to do a word study to see how they relate to us in English. The following is a presentation of Genesis 1:1-3 as found in the King James Version with the numbering system found in Strong's Exhaustive Concordance and definitions found in Young's Analytical Concordance.

Strongs #:	7225	430	1254
Hebrew Word:	RESHIYTH	ELOHIM	BARA
KJV words:	In the beginning	God	created

8064	776	776	1961
HAMAYIM	ERETS	ERETS	HAYAH
the heaven and	the earth.	And the earth	was

8414	922	2822	5921	6440
TOHUW	BOHUW	CHOSHEK	AL	PANAYIM
without form	and void;	and darkness	was upon	the face of

8415	7307	430	7363	5921
TEHOM	RUWACH	ELOHIM	RACHAPH	AL
the deep.	And the Spirit of	God	moved	upon

6440	4325	430	559	
PANAYIM	MAHIM	ELOHIM	AMAR	
the face of	the waters.	And God	said,	Let there

216	1961	216
OWR	HAYAH	OWR
be light and there	was	light.

Hebrew word	Strong's #	Young's Concordance
RESHIYTH	(7225)	the first, beginning, the chief
ELOHIM	(430)	God (plural), objects of worship
BARA	(1254)	to prepare, form, fashion, create
SHAMAYIM	(8064)	air, heaven (heaved up things)
ERETS	(776)	country, earth, ground
HAYAH	(1961)	to be, to become, to come to pass
TOHUW	(8414)	confusion, vanity, without form, ruin, vacancy

BOHUW	(922)	emptiness, void
CHOSHEK	(2822)	darkness
AL	(5921)	over, upon
PANAYIM	(6440)	face, countenance, presence
TEHOM	(8415)	deep, deep place, depth
RUWACH	(7307)	breath, spirit, wind
RACHAPH	(7363)	shake, flutter, move
MAYHIM	(4325)	water
AMAR	(559)	answer, command, speak, said
OWR	(216)	light

The YECs believe that all that is described in these three verses happened at the same time on what they believe was the first day of creation. The RTRs believe that verse 1 refers to the first act of <u>creation</u> bringing into existence the heaven and the earth. They further believe that something later happened to the earth to result in it becoming without form and void and having no life left upon it (which is referenced in verse 2). It was from that condition that verse 3 describes how God began the first of His four days work in making the Earth an inhabitable and beautiful place once again. He then <u>created</u> all life to dwell on it on days five and six.

The validity of one's belief can most often be determined by the validity of the evidence he uses to reach his conclusions. The only reason I have read or heard as to why YECs believe the first three verses must belong together, is that all the verses in Genesis 1 after the first begin with the conjunction "and". They believe, therefore, that it means that the events of one verse happened immediately after those of the previous verse.

I believe that it simply means that the latter events occurred some time after the former without implying how much later.

The RTRs have presented many reasons to believe what they do. I agree with them and will be sharing some of the biblical reasons that have helped them to reach their conclusions. As stated in the previous chapter, the beginning of the descriptions of what happened on days two through six all begin with the phrase *"And God said."* I believe that the description of the work done on day one begins in verse three because it starts with the very same phrase. Therefore, what is described in Genesis 1:1 and Genesis 1:2 occurred prior to the beginning of the six days work.

Difference in 'Created' and 'Made'

In Genesis 1:1, the word BARA is translated as 'created'. That word is not used again until the fifth day when Genesis 1:21 states *"And God created great whales."* No creative work is done on the first four days. Instead, the word ASAH is translated 'made' for the firmament (1:7) and the sun, moon and stars (1:16). The word BARA speaks of the act of God creating something out of nothing as described in Hebrews 11:3: *"Through faith we understand that the worlds were framed by the word of God, so that things which are seen were not made of things which do appear."* The word ASAH is used to describe the work of God in taking pre-existing material and changing it into another form.

On the first three days, the atmosphere, plants, water and land were all made from things already existing on the earth when it was without form and void. The water was divided, the dry land made to appear, and the seeds of grass and trees were already in themselves upon the earth. But, when God populated the newly renovated earth with fish, fowl, animals, and man, it required several acts of creation. Any creatures that lived upon the earth prior to it becoming without form and void had died long ago, so they had to be replaced.

The YECs teach that the two words BARA and ASAH are speaking of the same thing and can be used interchangeably. Once again, we must allow the Bible to interpret itself. If one believes in the verbally inspired Word of God (which I certainly do), then it is important to notice the words that God chose for Moses to use in leaving us the record of creation. When the six days work was finished, the following verses are found in Genesis 2:1-3: *"Thus the heavens and the earth were finished, and all the host of them. And on the seventh day God ended his work which he had MADE; and he rested on the seventh day from all his work which he had MADE. And God blessed the seventh day, and sanctified it: because that in it he had rested from all his work which God CREATED and MADE"* (Emphasis mine). If the two words mean the same, why did God use both of them in describing His work? They are not the same! Each word describes a separate work of God done on those six days.

Many who hold the view of the YECs also teach that the institution of the Sabbath proves that all of creation occurred on the six days. The Bible tells us to work six days and rest on the seventh, because God rested on the seventh day after His six days work. From that, they believe that everything

God has ever created or made was done on those six days. They ignore the fact, however, that the word 'create' is never used when speaking of the Sabbath. Instead, the word 'made' is used, *"For in six days the LORD made heaven and earth, the sea, and all that in them is, and rested the seventh day: wherefore the LORD blessed the sabbath day, and hallowed it"* (Exodus 20:11). Man was told to observe the Sabbath to honor the work of God done on the six days (Genesis 1:3-27) and has no reference to any creation prior to those days (Genesis 1:1).

God created the heaven and the earth in the beginning (whenever that was). On the fifth day, He created the fish and fowl. He completed His work of creation on the sixth day when He created creeping things, cattle, beasts, and man to dwell on the renewed earth. These are the only acts of creation that we are told about in Genesis 1.

The six days work involved God remaking the surface of the earth, establishing its new environment, and then creating new life to live on it: *"I have made (ASAH) the earth, and created (BARA) man upon it"* (Isaiah 45:12). Thus, it was God Himself who proves there is a difference in BARA and ASAH!

Creation of the Heaven

The Bible uses the word 'heaven' to speak of three different areas. The first heaven is the atmosphere where the birds fly (Jeremiah 4:25) and was made on the second day (Genesis 1:8). The second heaven speaks of the celestial area where the moon and all the stars and constellations exist (Isaiah 13:10). The third heaven is the place where the throne of God is located (Hebrews 9:24). The Apostle Paul was caught up to that third heaven: *"I knew a man in Christ above fourteen years ago, (whether in the body, I cannot tell; or whether out of the body, I cannot tell: God knoweth;) such an one caught up to the third heaven"* (2 Corinthians 12:2).

Since the first heaven (the atmosphere) was made on day two, it must be the second heaven with all of its celestial bodies that was created in the beginning as given in Genesis 1:1. We do not know when the third heaven had its beginning. Since it is the home of the eternal God, it has probably existed longer than the other two and is now the home of the redeemed of Adam's race who have died.

Now, the YECs believe that the sun, moon, and stars all came into being on the fourth day. If they are correct, then what was the heaven that was created in the beginning? Our word study reveals that the word for 'heaven' is SHAMAYIM and means 'heaved up things'. The Psalmist tells us what he considered the heavens to be: *"When I consider thy heavens, the work of thy fingers, the moon and the stars, which thou hast ordained"* (Psalm 8:3). He states that the heavens are the works of God's fingers and in the next phrase describes them as being the *'moon and the stars'*. Thus, they were created in the beginning but made (ASAH) to be suitable for the world of the new creation on the fourth day.

As the earth existed without form and void there was constant darkness over the entire planet. Evidently, the earth was covered by a thick cloud causing the state of darkness. We do not know the source of the light that God brought on the first day. The light may have come from His presence or He could have separated the darkness to allow the sunlight to touch the earth. It is obvious that something happened on day four when He commissioned the sun and moon to be a special influence for those who would be created to live on the earth: *"And God said, Let there be lights in the firmament of the heaven to divide the day from the night; and let them be for signs, and for seasons, and for days, and years"* (Genesis 1:14).

There was no work of creation on that day, but He could have changed the rotational speed of the earth about its axis, which would change the length of a day. He could have changed the orbit around the sun, which would affect the length of a year. The earth's axis is not perpendicular to the sun, but is at a 23 ½ ° angle. For one half of the year this causes the sun rays to directly strike the earth above the equator. That is our summer season. The rest of the year, the rays are below the equator and we go through our winter season. This tilt of the axis causes our four seasons and the signs that accompany their changes. This angle may have been different prior to the fourth day. All we know is that God ordained the sun and moon to be exactly what He knew that His new creation would need to be able to dwell upon this renovated earth.

The groups composed by the YECs and RTRs both give God credit for doing all things in the proper order. On the first four days, He gave light, provided the air of the atmosphere, divided land and sea, caused plants to grow, and assigned the sun and moon to their work. Then, He created living things to enjoy those things He had prepared. Everything was done in just the right order!

Since He does everything else in just the right order, why do the YECs believe that He would create the earth on the first day and wait until the fourth day to create the sun? It is the gravitational force of the sun that keeps the earth in orbit! What do they believe held the earth in place before the sun was created?

The RTRs have adequate reason to believe that the sun, moon, and stars were 'created' in the beginning, but 'made' to be the heavenly bodies that His new creation would need on the fourth day.

Creation of the Earth

The YECs believe that the earth came into existence during the six days work. They believe it was originally created 'without form and void' on day one and then it was fashioned into a beautiful and inhabited earth on the remaining days. They believe the earth has a very young age of just a few thousand years.

The RTRs believe that the earth could have been created a very long time ago but had come into the condition of being 'without form and void'. They see the possibility that the many fossil remains and geological formations that exist are remnants of the earth that existed prior to it becoming without form and void. The six days work is believed to be the work of God in renewing the face of the earth for His new created beings: *"Thou sendest forth thy spirit, they are created: and thou renewest the face of the earth"* (Psalm 104:30). They believe that it is possible that the earth as a planet could be very old.

It is my purpose to honestly present these divergent views. The two groups agree on the creation of all living creatures on earth and that they were all created just a few thousand years ago. They also agree on the reality of Noah's flood and some of the effects it may have had upon the planet. They just disagree on the condition of the earth in its original creation and when it occurred.

All the works of God are to perfection! It is totally inconsistent with the nature of God to believe He created the heavens perfectly but created the earth to be in a condition of being without form and void. If the earth was in that condition as a result of His creative act, it is the only thing you will ever find that was performed by God that was not done to perfection!

The word BARA is translated as 'created' and means to 'form and fashion'. The use of BARA is inconsistent with the condition of being 'without form' since it would mean to 'form without form'. In Wilson's Old Testament Word Studies, BARA is given the primary meaning, "The production or effectuation of something new, rare, and wonderful; the bringing something to pass in a striking and marvelous manner". It should be evident that a condition of being 'without form and void' is NOT a result of God's creation!

The angels were created before the creation of the earth. They had seen so many other things that were the works of God's hands, but they were overcome with awe when they saw the earth as God first laid its foundation. God described their reaction to Job: *Where wast thou when I laid the foundations of the earth? declare, if thou hast understanding. Who hath laid the measures thereof, if thou knowest? or who hath stretched the line upon it? Whereupon are the foundations thereof fastened? or who laid the corner stone thereof; When the morning stars sang together, and all the sons of God shouted for joy?"* (Job 38:4-7). This was not a reference to the six days work, but when the foundation was laid. Would they have been so awe struck at an earth without form and void? When they first saw it, the earth must have been like a shining diamond compared to the rest of creation!

The earth had already been created when Lucifer rebelled against God. In Isaiah's account of his rebellion, he said, *"For thou hast said in thine heart, I will ascend into heaven, I will exalt my throne above the stars of God: I will sit also upon the mount of the congregation, in the sides of the north: I will ascend above the heights of the clouds; I will be like the most High"* (Isaiah 14:13, 14). Where was he when he said he would ascend into heaven and above the clouds? He had to have been on the earth! Jesus saw what took place as a result of this sin: *"And he said unto them, I beheld Satan as lightning fall from heaven"* (Luke 10:18). Again, where was he falling to if not the earth? It seems evident that Lucifer had already rebelled and been cast down prior to Adam and Eve being in the Garden of Eden.

The RTRs believe that the judgment of God began to fall on the earth after the rebellious Lucifer had been cast down as Satan. I believe that Lucifer once had a special relationship with a beautiful earth and was most likely the one who God appointed to reign over it. Some reasons for this belief will be fully discussed in later chapters. After he fell as lightning from heaven following his rebellion, judgments began to fall on the earth. The judgments were not brought by him, but by God as He judged the first sin that had ever been committed against Him. Lucifer had dared to try to be like God, but he made a very poor god. He was unable to do anything to stop the judgments or keep the earth from becoming 'without form and void'. It may have taken millions or billions of years of cataclysmic judgments before the earth became as described in Genesis 1:2.

In like manner, when Adam and Eve sinned, the earth was cursed once again. The earth has already gone through many judgments such as the flood of Noah's day, storms, volcanoes, earthquakes, etc. It is now headed toward the Great Tribulation which will be the final wrath of God upon this earth before it is destroyed by fire. The only thing that will save earth from becoming a lifeless planet 'without form and void' again is the fact that Jesus will come to bring the Tribulation to an end: *"And except those days should be shortened, there should no flesh be saved: but for the elect's sake those days shall be shortened"* (Matthew 24:22).

<u>What It Was, It Became</u>

In Genesis 1:1 we are told about the creation of the heaven and the earth. Then, in verse two we find the words *"the earth was without form and void."* The YECs believe that this describes the earth as it was created. The RTRs believe that it describes the condition of the earth at a later time after it was created and may or may not be an accurate description of its created condition. The difference in opinion is of paramount importance if we are to adequately determine the possible age of the earth.

The word 'was' is a form of the verb 'to be'. It describes a state of being as one looks back on a moment in the past. It can correctly be stated that the Mississippi Gulf Coast 'was' in a devastated condition on August 30, 2005. Two days prior to that date, however, it was in a beautiful condition. It was hurricane Katrina that made the difference! The word 'was' in verse two simply describes the condition of the earth at that point in time without implying that it had been created that way, or that it had always been that way since being created.

The word HAYAH is most often translated as 'was' in the Scriptures, but it is also translated as 'became' or 'become'. The following verses present some of those places:

> "And the LORD God formed man of the dust of the ground, and breathed into his nostrils the breath of life; and man became (HAYAH) a living soul" (Genesis 2:7)

> "But his wife looked back from behind him, and she became (HAYAH) a pillar of salt" (Genesis 19:26)

> "And yet indeed she is my sister; she is the daughter of my father, but not the daughter of my mother; and she became (HAYAH) my wife" (Genesis 20:12)

> "The stone which the builders refused is become (HAYAH) the head stone of the corner" (Psalm 118:22)

There are also numerous places where the word is translated 'was' when it is obvious that it is describing a condition that resulted from a recent change. If we limit ourselves to the verses following Genesis 1:2 we can prove that to be true. For example, "And God said, Let there be light: and there was (HAYAH) light" (Genesis 1:3). There was darkness before God spoke but then there became light. In Genesis 1:7, 9, 11, 15, 24, and 30, the words are found "and it was (HAYAH) so."

The honest reader must agree that those verses could have been accurately translated "and it became so" if the translators had chosen to do so.

The YECs are adamant in their claim that the word 'was' CANNOT be understood to mean 'became'. Hopefully, the examples given above are enough to prove to the reader that it is certainly a possibility. One has to wonder if the KJV had been translated "And the earth became without form and void" if there would be so much resistance to the belief that the original earth had gone through great judgments prior to its renovation in the six days.

The Condition Of Being Without Form and Void

The Greek words TOHUW and BOHUW give us the words 'without form and void'. The word TOHUW describes a condition of ruin while BOHUW is revealing emptiness. Both of these words are used separately in the original language in numerous places, but they are found together (as in Genesis 1:2) in only two other texts.

> "For it is the day of the LORD'S vengeance, and the year of recompenses for the controversy of Zion. And the streams thereof shall be turned into pitch, and the dust thereof into brimstone, and the land thereof shall become burning pitch. It shall not be quenched night nor day; the smoke thereof shall go up for ever: from generation to generation it shall lie waste; none shall pass through it for ever and ever. But the cormorant and the bittern shall possess it; the owl also and the raven shall dwell in it: and he shall stretch out upon it the line of confusion (TOHUW), and the stones of emptiness (BOHUW) " (Isaiah 34:8-11)

"I beheld the earth, and, lo, it was without form (TOHUW), and void (BOHUW); and the heavens, and they had no light. I beheld the mountains, and, lo, they trembled, and all the hills moved lightly. I beheld, and, lo, there was no man, and all the birds of the heavens were fled. I beheld, and, lo, the fruitful place was a wilderness, and all the cities thereof were broken down at the presence of the LORD, and by his fierce anger. For thus hath the LORD said, The whole land shall be desolate; yet will I not make a full end" (Jeremiah 4:23-27)

Isaiah was speaking about a coming day when God would bring about the condition of TOHUW and BOHUW that is translated 'line of confusion and stones of emptiness'. This condition would be brought about because *"it is the day of God's vengeance and the year of recompenses for the controversy of Zion."* Without question, it is the judgment and wrath of God that would bring about that condition.

It seems that Jeremiah was given a vision of what had happened to the earth to make it TOHUW and BOHUW. Many deny this, believing that Jeremiah was giving a prophecy concerning Judah before the Babylonian captivity. There are two reasons I reject their view. Jeremiah did not say he saw Judah, but he saw the earth! Also, although Judah was destroyed by the Babylonians, they were never in the condition of being without form and void. Regardless, Jeremiah saw the condition of TOHUW and BOHUW and clearly states it was the result of being *"broken down at the presence of the LORD, and by his fierce anger."*

The two words are found together in only three places. In two of those texts, it is obvious that they describe a destruction and emptiness brought about by the anger, wrath and judgment of a holy God. Does this require one to believe that the third text (Genesis 1:2) must also be accepted as describing the condition and effects of the judgment of God? Not necessarily. But, it certainly doesn't rule out the possibility! If one allows the Bible to interpret itself, then credence must be given to the possibility that the *"without form and void"* described in Genesis 1:2 is not speaking of God's creative abilities, but the results of His judgment against sin!

The Earth As Originally Created

It has been shown that the word 'was' could be correctly understood as meaning 'became'. The use of the words TOHUW and BOHUW describing the 'without form and void' condition of the earth has been shown to reveal the possible effects of God's judgments. If we had a verse that described the condition of the earth immediately after it was created in Genesis 1:1 it would help us to know if a change had occurred before the next verse. We may have such a verse!

> *"For thus saith the LORD that created the heavens; God himself that formed the earth and made it; he hath established it, he created it not in vain* (TOHUW), *he formed it to be inhabited: I am the LORD; and there is none else"* (Isaiah 45:18)

You will notice that God first speaks about creating the heavens. Then, He tells that He 'formed the earth and made it' as He described what happened in the six days. In each case in this verse the word 'formed' was translated from YATSAR which means to "squeeze into shape or mold into a form as by a potter."

He then states that He *"created it not in vain"*. The word translated as 'vain' is the same TOHUW that was translated 'without form' in Genesis 1:2. By substituting the previous translation of TOHUW, we have "He created it not without form, he formed it to be inhabited." If it was not created without form then it had to have become without form at some time after creation! Thus, we know that in the beginning it was created perfectly to be inhabited, but after judgment had made it uninhabitable it had to be formed and made over again.

<u>The Command To Replenish The Earth</u>

During the work of six days, the earth was prepared for habitation and God created man and all the new creatures to enjoy the beauty of His work. It was then that He gave a special command to Adam: *"And God blessed them, and God said unto them, Be fruitful, and multiply, and replenish the earth"* (Genesis 1:28a). The YECs contend that the word 'replenish' simply means to 'fill'. The RTRs see the possibility that it could mean to 'fill it again'. Only God knows what He really meant because the Hebrew word MALE that was translated could have either of these meanings. It would be helpful if the Lord would tell us what He meant. Maybe He did!

After the flood, Noah, his wife, his three sons and their wives were the only humans left to live on the earth. It would be up to those three sons to repopulate the earth with Adam's descendants. God gave Noah a special command: *"And God blessed Noah and his sons, and said unto them, Be fruitful, and multiply, and replenish the earth"* (Genesis 9:1). The three Hebrew words that were used in the command to Adam were

PARAH RABAH MALE, meaning 'fruitful, multiply, replenish'. The same exact words were used in the command to Noah. We know that He was telling Noah to 'fill it again'!

If the Bible is allowed to interpret itself, then proper consideration must be given to the possibility (and maybe even probability) that God was telling Adam to 'fill it again'. It would be the first time for Adam and his race, but not the first time for God to see an inhabited earth!

⁓

Some biblical reasons that cause the RTRs to believe in the ruin and restoration of the earth have been presented. Their beliefs are based on the Bible, not on any scientific discoveries! Any discovery made in the past, or any that may be made in the future, can be explained and understood when one sees the earth as having a great and long history.

Many things happened on earth before it became without form and void. The earth has experienced many things since the six days work. God has been there all the time! He is glorified through it all! Thus far, there has been only one earth, though many worlds (or ages) may have existed on it. Notice the following verses that speak of the creation.

"Hath in these last days spoken unto us by his Son, whom he hath appointed heir of all things, by whom also he made the worlds" (Hebrews 1:2)

"Through faith we understand that the worlds were framed by the word of God, so that things which are seen were not made of things which do appear" (Hebrews 11:3)

In these verses the word 'worlds' is plural speaking of more than one world (or age) that He has made. In each case, the word translated 'worlds' is from the Greek word AION and means age or dispensation. In contrast, the Greek word KOSMOS was translated as 'world' in John 3:16 and Romans 5:12 and is often related to mankind on earth.

As first pointed out, the best interpreter of the Bible is the Bible itself. While no person can be dogmatic in describing how God created the universe, it seems apparent that the earth was created as an absolutely perfect creation that later became "without form and void." This state of ruin must have come about as a result of Lucifer being cast from Heaven to the earth and the consequential judgments. My belief that these statements are true came about by allowing the Bible to interpret itself. I encourage all readers to study God's perfect, infallible and inerrant Word to confirm (or deny) these teachings (Acts 17:11). The next two chapters will study the sins of Lucifer and Adam and present how their respective sins affected the earth.

Chapter 3
WHAT EARTH HAS TO SAY

The eternal God was present when the earth was created! What He has to say about it is very important. The earth has been here since that time and it would be helpful if it could talk and tell us all about what has happened since creation. Well, its voice may be silent, but it still has a lot to say, and we need to be listening.

Any human body has signs that tell us much about what has happened to that body. A strand of hair can reveal what drugs have been present in the body in the last three months. A simple blood test of a diabetic can show his or her average sugar level for the past three months. Modern medicine can find many things that have happened to a body in the past by looking at its current condition. It should be no surprise that the earth is also filled with information about its history.

Jesus also taught that the earth can tell us what may happen in the immediate future: *"He answered and said unto them, When it is evening, ye say, It will be fair weather: for the sky is red. And in the morning, It will be foul weather to day: for the sky is red and lowring"* (Matthew 16:2, 3a). Many things that have happened on earth in the past have left signs of their occurrences as well.

We just need to be able to read those signs accurately and then we will be able to hear what the earth has to say.

Many scientists have spent much time studying about the earth in the various fields of geology, archaeology, astronomy, anthropology, physics, chemistry, biology, etc. Most scientists have analytical minds and are like good detectives – they only go where the evidence takes them. They do not set out to prove or disprove the Bible. They only want to look at all that has been discovered and try to find rational answers to understand the universe. The major part of their evidence is found on earth because that is where they live and work. They try to use the information discovered on earth to better understand the solar system and the rest of the universe.

The YECs consider their belief that all things were created just 6,000 years ago to be a fact and not a theory. Since they consider it an established fact that the earth has a very young age, they must then find an explanation as to why so much of the scientific evidence seems to speak of millions or billions of years, and not just thousands. Some YECs believe that maybe God created the earth with an appearance of being very old. Others see the signs of many calamities on the earth and give the flood of Noah's day the credit for doing the vast majority of the damage. Most of their explanations are taken from *"The Genesis Flood"* written by John C. Whitcomb and Henry M. Morris in 1961.

In this chapter, I will present many quotes from this book. Although it had two authors, most refer to Morris as being the main author, so for brevity's sake I will do the same. Since it is the original reference book for the YECs, I felt obligated to read the entire book myself so that I could accurately and honestly report from it. Morris did an excellent job of presenting the scientific discoveries that have been made concerning earth's history <u>that make it to appear very old</u>. Yet, when Morris tried to explain everything as occurring recently, I considered most of his "proofs" to have come from an active imagination. Furthermore, he continually spoke of what possibly could have happened that most true scientists would totally reject.

Morris began with an assumption that the earth is only a few thousand years old and tried to find evidence that would validate his belief. If the evidence found on earth did not prove what he believed, then he tried to discredit it by generating possibilities that the evidence was not accurate. Apparently he never considered the possibility that his understanding of the biblical account of creation was not accurate!

<u>A Canopy Over The Earth Before the Flood</u>

To explain how the flood came about, Morris presented the possibility that there was a canopy of water over the entire earth prior to the flood. This would have provided enough 'water from above' for the earth to be covered.

> As we have seen, these waters apparently existed in the form of a great vapor canopy around the earth, of unknown but possibly very great extent. As vapor, it was quite invisible but, nevertheless, would have had a profound effect on terrestrial climate and meteorological processes.[5]

Morris further claimed that this would cause a warm climate all over the earth and would inhibit winds from fronts brought about by changing weather. In turn, he states that men lived longer since the rays from the sun were filtered out.

One problem I have with this hypothesis is that on day four God made the sun and moon so they would cause the earth to have seasons and signs. This canopy would have hindered the seasons from coming. Man's life span was shortened because of sin and not because of the sun's rays. When Jesus returns to reign on earth for 1,000 years in a kingdom of peace, the life span of man will be greatly increased again: *"There shall be no more thence an infant of days, nor an old man that hath not filled his days: for the child shall die an hundred years old; but the sinner being an hundred years old shall be accursed. — for as the days of a tree are the days of my people, and mine elect shall long enjoy the work of their hands"* (Isaiah 65:20, 22b). Human life span will not be increased because of a canopy over the earth, but because Jesus is reigning as King of kings in a righteous kingdom!

The YECs have tried to use this canopy theory to prove their other theories, but admit that the vapor canopy would not have contained enough water to make much difference. Ken Ham expressed this view.

> Canopy theory. This is not a direct teaching of Scripture, so there is no place for dogmatism. Also, no suitable model has been developed that holds sufficient water; but some creationists suggest a partial canopy may have been present.[6]

It is obvious from Scripture that *"the same day were all the fountains of the great deep broken up, and the windows of heaven were opened"* (Genesis 7:11) to provide all the water necessary for the flood. This is not something that can be duplicated or explained, but an act of judgment by an angry God. The Bible does not teach about a canopy, nor have scientific discoveries revealed that it ever existed, so I reject it as a possibility. Morris, himself, admitted that there was no proof.

> Although we can as yet point to no definite scientific verification of this pristine vapor protective envelope around the earth, neither does there appear to be any inherent physical difficulty in the hypothesis of its existence, and it does suffice to explain a broad spectrum of phenomena both geological and Scriptural.[7]

He admitted there was no proof, yet in many other places in his book, he used the supposed existence of a canopy to explain how other things happened.

Cataclysms That Have Touched The Earth

The geological formations that are found throughout the earth's surface have led many to believe that the earth has gone through some great cataclysmic changes. There have been times when it must have appeared that the planet would be destroyed as convulsions and shakings occurred. Morris also believes this is true as he shared in his discussions about the strata that make up the earth.

> But nothing ever seen by man in the present era can compare with whatever the phenomena were which caused the formation of these tremendous structures. — Great thicknesses of rocks have apparently been uplifted thousands of feet; strata have buckled, folded, sometimes been thrust laterally or completely overturned on a gigantic scale. — The crust of the

earth seems to have been distorted, fractured, elevated, depressed and contorted in almost every conceivable way at some time or times in the past.[8]

Each of the important geologic processes, without exception, must at some time or times in the geologic past, have acted with tremendously greater intensity than anything measured today. Present day volcanic activity is not only quantitatively but qualitatively different from the volcanic phenomena of the geologic past that have produced the great dikes and sills, the batholiths and laccoliths, as well as the great lava fields and plateaus of the world.[9]

While admitting that what the earth has to say about its geological past can not be understood by anything that is occurring today, Morris believed that there were five times when events have taken place on the earth to leave evidence of great cataclysmic activity.[10]

1. The Initial Creation Itself.
2. The Work of the Six Days of Creation
3. The Antediluvian Period (time before the flood)
4. The Deluge (the flood itself)
5. The Modern Post-Deluge Period

According to Morris, all the fierce activity that has left so many geological records on earth occurred during these times. Yet, he and apparently all the YECs believe that the greatest changes occurred in the time of Noah's flood.

The Bible describes what happened when the waters covered the earth: *"In the six hundredth year of Noah's life, in the second month, the seventeenth day of the month, the same day were all the fountains of the great deep broken up, and the windows of heaven were opened"* (Genesis 7:11). The water began to fall from above as all the waters beneath the earth's surface were forced to the surface. These two sources of water continued until the Lord stopped their actions: *"The fountains also of the deep and the windows of heaven were stopped, and the rain from heaven was restrained; And the waters returned from off the earth continually: and after the end of the hundred and fifty days the waters were abated"* (Genesis 8:2, 3).

Morris taught that when the 'fountains of the great deep' were broken up it was <u>possibly</u> caused by great earthquakes and volcanoes all over the earth. These would have caused great tsunamis over the earth that totally changed the topography.

> Tsunamis have been known to attain velocities of 400 or more miles per hour and heights of 130 feet and to travel extraordinary distances. – And it is just this most destructive of all types of waves which must have been produced during the Biblical flood by the "breaking up of the fountains of the great deep"! Furthermore, this break-up, with all its attendant destructiveness, apparently continued from the first day of the Flood (Genesis 7:11) through the same period as the great rains from heaven, until both were stopped by God (Genesis 8:2).[11]

What Morris presented in his book as a <u>possibility</u> is now being taught by the YECs as a fact. His son, Dr. John Morris, is Director of the Institute of Creation Research that was founded by his father. He continues to present his father's view as revealed in the following article taken from his web site, but he presents it as a fact and not a possibility.

> Noah and his family had just come through an unimaginable frightening experience. Perhaps they had never even seen a storm, and certainly no one had ever seen one like this. It would have been indelibly impressed on their memories. During the Flood, the winds incessantly howled, the thunder continually pealed as the Ark pitched and rolled in the waves. Earthquakes shook the planet without stop, sending pulsating tsunamis in every direction. Underwater volcanoes and the spreading "fountains of the great deep" (Genesis 7:11) heated the water surrounding the Ark, making life on board almost unbearable. And the never ceasing rainfall so pelted the Ark's roof it was like being under Niagara Falls.[12]

The Bible does not tell us what life was like inside the ark. It also doesn't describe all the activity outside the ark that the YECs believe and teach! But, because they base all their beliefs on the earth having only been here for a few thousand years, they have to come up with some explanation for the catastrophes that have definitely occurred at some time. Obviously, people can choose to believe what they want, but that does not make those beliefs true.

The source of all the water during the flood resulted from God's actions and cannot be explained by natural phenomena. He caused all the water from beneath to come forth as many springs and fountains do today. The ark was simply lifted up by the waters. Noah and his family did not huddle together in the ark in fear as it was tossed about by tsunamis. I am convinced that there was a total calm inside the ark because Noah had built it by faith, and he would wait in confident faith for God's judgment to be over. He knew that everything would be well for him and his family. The animals all rested in complete solitude and were not being bounced around from the ark being tossed to and fro. I choose to believe all of that! I do not believe it because it helps prove that the earth has been here for a long time, but because the gracious God we know would not invite Noah's family and all the animals into the ark of salvation and then treat them in such a way!

I do acknowledge there have been many judgments on the earth since the six days work because of God's judgment on Adam's original sin. The storms, earthquakes, volcanoes, etc., that have occurred were direct results of the curse that was brought on the earth. Other judgments have come as a result of the sin of people who were living on earth at that particular time. When Korah rebelled against Moses, the earth opened up to swallow all of his family, their homes, and all that pertained to them (Numbers 16:31-33). After Lot's family had left Sodom and Gomorrah, God rained fire and brimstone down upon those wicked cities and evidently lifted them and turned them upside down back on the earth (Genesis 19:24, 25). Surely there have been many more individual judgments because of similar sins, but it all goes back to the curse placed on the earth because of Adam's sin in the garden. I believe greater catastrophes are coming.

Jesus, teaching about the coming Great Tribulation, promised that great judgments would come to earth involving earthquakes: *"For nation shall rise against nation, and kingdom against kingdom: and there shall be famines, and pestilences, and earthquakes, in divers places"* (Matthew 24:7). As that period of time is described in the book of Revelation, earthquakes are repeatedly mentioned (Revelation 6:12, 8:5; 11:13, 19). These will not be earthquakes like we have known before. In Revelation 6:14 we are told, *"every mountain and island were moved out of their places"*. Also, in Revelation 8:8, *"as it were a great mountain burning with fire was cast into the sea"*. These will not be isolated earthquakes, but many will be occurring all over the earth at the same time. When Jesus said *"in divers places"* He meant in diverse or different places. Many changes will be made on the topography of the earth in those last days.

God spoke through the prophet Zechariah of the changes that will occur around Jerusalem when the feet of Jesus touch the earth. In Zechariah 14:4, He said the Mount of Olives will split apart with part of it moving to the north and part to the south providing a deep valley between. In verse eight of that same chapter, God stated that living waters would flow down that valley with some towards the Mediterranean Sea and some to the Dead Sea. He continued in verse ten by stating that all the land around Jerusalem would become a plain. Today, Jerusalem sits on top of a mountain range, but that will all change at the conclusion of the Tribulation period.

The geological formations of the earth do prove that this planet has gone through some tremendous cataclysmic upheavals at some time in the past as Morris claims. The RTRs also believe that the flood, other storms, earthquakes, volcanoes, tsunamis, etc., have left an imprint on the earth, but not nearly enough to explain all the available evidence. Thus, they believe that much (if not most) of the damage that has been done to the earth happened prior to it becoming 'without form and void', and this was long before the flood ever occurred.

The Bible is written to give us a record of God's dealing with man since the six days work. It doesn't tell us much of what He was doing prior to that time. But, if one believes in the verbally inspired Word of God, then every word and phrase found in the Bible is of significance. God doesn't waste words. He inspired the Apostle John to describe the final earthquake that will occur at the end of the Great Tribulation period: *"There was a great earthquake, such as was not since men were upon the earth, so mighty an earthquake, and so great"* (Revelation 16:18). There must be a reason why God made the designation "since men were upon the earth." If men were created with the original earth, the statement would have no meaning. But, if there were even more terrible earthquakes because of Lucifer's sin than what has happened thus far because of the sin of Adam, then the statement makes perfect sense.

The earth does show signs of tremendous earthquakes at some times in the past that were far more cataclysmic than any that have occurred since the six days work. The earthquake described above will be the greatest since men were upon the earth and may be comparable to those that brought the destruction that resulted in the earth becoming without form and void.

Formation of Sedimentary Rocks And Fossil Graveyards

Sedimentary rocks are given that name because it is believed that sediments were used to form them. As water washed mud and silt into an area, the water eventually evaporated and the dry minerals were left. As more materials covered them later, the dry minerals became rock. The following information comes from *The World Book Encyclopedia*.

> Sedimentary rock is formed when mineral matter settles out of water, or, less commonly, out of air or ice. Sedimentary rock covers about three-fourths of the earth's land area. In some places, such as at the mouth of the Mississippi River, sedimentary rocks are more than 40,000 feet thick. — The most common sedimentary rock is shale or mudstone. It is made of compressed mud or silt (fine particles of mineral matter). Other common sedimentary rocks include limestone, made of the mineral calcite, and sandstone, made of sand. — Most fossils are found in sedimentary rock. The fossils formed when sediments covered dead plants and animals.[13]

When Morris described the formation of sedimentary rock, he basically presented the same information.

> Most of the sedimentary rocks of the earth's crust, which are the ones containing fossil remains and which therefore provide the chief basis of geologic interpretation of earth history, have been laid down as sediments by moving water (some have apparently been formed by wind, glaciers, or other agencies, but by far the largest part of sedimentary rocks are aqueous in origin). It is even possible that many metamorphic (including "granitized" rocks, ordinarily classed as igneous) were originally sedimentaries.

> Sedimentary rocks have been formed through a process of erosion, transportation, deposition, and lithification

of sediments. The deposition occurs, of course, when the running water containing the sediments enters a quiescent or less rapidly moving body of water, the lowered velocity resulting in a dropping out of part or all of its load of moving sediment. If the sediment happens to contain organic remains, and these are buried by the sands or silts accompanying them, it may be possible over the years for the organic remains to become fossilized and be preserved in form in the stratum. The remains of such plant and animal forms, as discovered in the present sedimentary rocks of the earth, have of course served as the basis of our modern divisions of the strata into units of geologic time.[14]

We have all observed the results of the work of sedimentation when we have seen the stripes in rocks, layers of different colors and materials on the side of a cliff, or layers of different material discovered when digging in the ground. To believe that God created the earth with these identifying marks, one would have to believe that He also placed the various fossil remains in each of the layers at the time of creation.

When a dinosaur walked in wet sediment, it would of course leave large footprints. If the prints were not obliterated, they could eventually be covered by dry material that would allow the sediment to become rock so they would be preserved. If the remains of other creatures were in the sediment, the identifying shapes of each creature would be found in the rock even if the bodies themselves were decayed.

It is the presence of different types of plants and fossils in the various layers of sedimentary rock in the same area that has led to the development of the geologic ages. Different birds, reptiles, insects, etc., have been found in successive layers causing geologists to believe that a long time existed between the times when some of the rocks were made. Thus, the Geologic Time Table was developed whereby the history of earth was divided into five periods of time – Archeozoic, Proterozoic, Paleozoic, Mesozoic, and Cenozoic. Cenozoic is the time in which we are living with the others being successively older.

Morris believed that most of the layers of sedimentary rocks that contained fossils were all developed by catastrophic activity on the earth and not by normal processes.

> We have shown that some kind of catastrophic condition is nearly always necessary for the burial and preservation of fossils. Present day processes are forming very few potential fossil deposits, and most of these are under conditions of rapid, sudden burial, which are abnormal. Nothing comparable to the tremendous fossiliferous beds of fish, mammals, reptiles, etc. that are found in many places around the world is being formed today.[15]

I agree with him totally, except that he believes the flood was the one catastrophe that made the successive layers as waves of water piled them on top of one another. The earth had to have known many catastrophes over a long period of time before it ever became without form and void. For the sediments to become rocks that contained fossils, a long period of time was required between the cataclysmic activities. Successive waves of wet debris piled on top of one another would not make the layers of rock formations that exist.

There was a lot of volcanic activity that caused great damage to the earth prior to the six days work. Morris presented evidence that the ash from volcanoes became rock that contained many fossils.

An entirely different type of deposit, but one also containing a wealth of fossils, is that near Florissant, Colorado, where myriads of a wide variety of insect fossils are preserved in rocks of volcanic shale, with a minute perfection of detail that is truly remarkable, interspersed with layers of other types of fossils.[16]

Morris referenced the following article that gives great detail regarding many volcanoes that had erupted in the same area at some time in the past and the evidence that exists to give us an idea of earth's history.[17]

In Yellowstone Park there is a stratigraphic section of 2000 feet exposed which shows 18 successive petrified forests. Each forest grew to maturity before it was wiped out with a lava flow. The lava had to be weathered into soil before the next forest could even start. Further, this is only a small section stratigraphic column in this area.[18]

He also referenced another article about a similar, if not the same, formation on Amethyst Mountain and Specimen Ridge.

On the slopes of Amethyst Mountain 15 successive forests are exposed, one above the other, and each is separated from the next one above or below by a few inches or feet of ash.[19]

The evidence seems very clear and obvious that successive volcanoes erupted in the same area burying one forest after another. There had to be enough time between the eruptions for top soil to form and a new forest to grow. These occurred over a long period of time and contributed to the earth becoming without form and void. But, Morris believed the flood did it all.

> The stumps give every appearance of having been in some manner sheared off by some overwhelming force (possibly tsunami driven debris), then uprooted and transported and sorted out from other materials and then suddenly buried beneath a volcanic shower. Then came another wave of sediment and stumps (several layers of sediment, however, appear to be without stumps), possibly resulting from the tsunami generated by the preceding eruption, then another volcanic shower, and so on. The whole formation, as does the volcanic terrain all over the Yellowstone region and the Pacific northwest, literally proclaims catastrophic deposition![20]

Thus, Morris' theory of the presence of tsunamis during the flood is now used to explain over 2,000 feet of volcanic destruction. In these areas, numerous petrified trees are standing out of the ground where they once grew. It would be difficult to explain how tsunamis stood trees upright after washing them into an area! This strange type of logic is used throughout his book.

<u>Deposits of Coal and Petroleum</u>

Everyone seems to agree that coal came from plants and trees that were buried beneath the earth. The imprint of individual leaves and other identifying things found in coal can leave no doubt. It is also agreed that petroleum comes from decaying animal and plant life. The time period that would be required for these great sources of energy to be deposited, however, is a matter of disagreement.

Morris presented the fact that a vast amount of plant life would be required to form a seam of coal. He also acknowledged the tremendous amount of coal that is buried beneath the earth. What he presented is consistent with other sources.

> The coal deposits of the world are of course tremendous in magnitude, with the exact amount quite uncertain, but somewhere around 7 trillion tons. — Each foot of coal must represent many feet – just how many, no one knows – of plant remains, so that the coal measures testify of the former existence of almost unimaginably massive accumulations of buried plants. — There are many sites where 75 or more such coal seams are found. Some seams, too, are up to 30 or 40 feet in thickness, representing perhaps an accumulation of 300 or 400 feet of plant remains for the one seam.[21]

He also believed that all the large reservoirs of petroleum that exist beneath the surface of the earth were put there by the decomposition of plants and animals.

> The exact nature of the organic material has been as yet quite unsettled, but there seems little doubt that the vast reservoirs of organic remains, both plant and animal, in the sedimentary rocks constitute a more than adequate source. — The general picture of vast organic remains, somehow dissolved and transformed chemically into petroleum hydrocarbons, then eventually

reprecipitated as oil, is basically valid and harmonizes well with the concept of catastrophic burial and dissolution during the Deluge.[22]

Notice that by mentioning the Deluge (Noah's flood) Morris claimed that all the deposits were made about 4,000 years ago. He also believed that all the seams of coal stacked one upon another were placed there by the great waves of the tsunamis.

We know that reservoirs of oil are found almost all over the earth beneath every continent, even the North Pole. It is also true that coal has been found beneath the earth's surface basically all around the earth. Morris believed that the Deluge occurred just a few thousand years after the first plants and animals were created. Further, he believes that there were enough animals killed and plants buried in the flood to produce all the petroleum and coal that has been discovered. To accept his teachings, one would also have to believe that 4,000 years is sufficient time for all the plants and animals to be transformed into petroleum and coal.

I realize that God could have created the earth with all the coal and oil deposits already in it. That would be much more reasonable and believable than what the YECs believe. However, I believe they are there because they were being stored when God was judging Lucifer's sin by bringing many cataclysmic catastrophes upon the earth. So when I hear someone talking about the coal and oil being in the earth for millions of years, I do not disagree with them – I just thank God for providing it for us to use in these last days of the earth!

Changing Speed of Light

One of the disagreements between the RTRs and YECs concerns how the light rays from the stars that are several hundred thousand light years away from the earth have reached earth in 6,000 years. A light year is the distance that light travels in one year at the rate of 186,000 miles per second. It has been estimated that the light we see from earth's nearest star left that star around the time that Columbus discovered America. Yet, the farthest stars from earth are estimated to be millions of light years away.

Morris presented his view that when God created the stars on the fourth day He also created the light rays so they reached earth at the same time.

> The photons of light energy were created at the same instant as the stars from which they were apparently derived, so that an observer on the earth would have been able to see the most distant stars within his vision at that instant of creation. There is nothing unreasonable either philosophically or scientifically in this.[23]

Most YECs have adopted his view in an effort to make their teachings believable that the stars and earth were created at the same time just 6,000 years ago. There is no doubt that God has the power to do that very thing, but did He?

Sometimes a star will explode leaving a huge display in the sky. This is called a supernova. In 1987, a star that had been observed and measured as being over 150,000 light years away suddenly exploded leaving a large area of debris that was visible to the astronomers. Now, if the YECs theory is true then that star never existed! God would have had to create a ray that was

6,000 light years long, and then create a large number of light rays to reveal the debris, but the star itself would have never existed!

It should be evident that if a star was 150,000 light years away and its explosion was observed on earth it would mean the star had been in existence for at least 150,000 years. But, Answers In Genesis (AIG), which was organized by Ken Ham who became a YEC after reading Morris book *The Genesis Flood*, came up with an explanation for us.

> First, you have assumed that light has always traveled at the same speed. Second, you have assumed that the effects of gravitational time dilation are insignificant. Under the right conditions, light from the most distant galaxies could have arrived at earth in very short amounts of time. Third, you have assumed (without justification) a particular synchrony convention. The terrestrial equivalent of this fallacy would be assuming that noon in London, England, is the same as noon in Cincinnati, Ohio. Fourth, and perhaps most importantly, you have assumed that the light arrived entirely by natural means. Such reasoning is no different than those who reject the resurrection of Christ because it cannot be explained by natural forces. However, God created the stars supernaturally during Creation Week and made them to give light upon earth. Since this happened during Creation Week, God may have used different means to get distant starlight here than the "natural" means by which He upholds the universe today.[24]

Now, if you are scratching your head after reading his explanation, you are not alone! To show that they really teach this,

I want to share more information on this subject from another article written by Ham.[25] The writer states there are five possible areas of explanation in his opinion that are all consistent with the text of Genesis. The second and third are almost identical so I will only present four areas.

1. The language of Genesis is phenomenological language (describing appearance). In this case, stars were made millions and billions of years before Day 4, but in such a manner that the light from all stars, no matter how far away all arrived at the earth on Day 4 and so would have been seen first at that moment.

2. That clocks in the cosmos in the past have run at much higher rates than clocks on earth. Especially during Creation Week, clocks of the exact same type on the edge of the universe ran something like 10^{13} times faster than clocks on earth and therefore light from such regions had plenty of time to get to earth in a matter of days, not millions or billions of years.

3. That the speed of light was enormously faster in the past, of the order 10^{11} to 10^{12} c. This may have been the case during Creation Week and then the light slowed enormously to the present value.

4. Mystery and miracles! This last option I have to include because the Creator God revealed in the Bible *is* a God of miracles. It is probably true that if we were looking a miracle in the face we might try to reason a naturalistic mechanism for it. For example, when supernova 1987A exploded in the Large Magellanic Cloud, did it explode 200,000 years ago or in 1987? God could

have miraculously translated the light across 200,000 light years distance of space instantly (as if the photons passed through a wormhole) and then just outside the solar system let it move at the speed *c*.

It causes me great concern that AIG in the name of Jesus Christ is teaching such imaginations as this and innocent people are just accepting it as the truth! The speed of light (c) is 186,000 miles per second, but they say that in Creation Week you can add either 11 or 12 zeroes on to the end of that rate. This is just one of the many fallacies of their teaching that prove beyond doubt that the YECs have no basis for their beliefs either biblically or scientifically.

<u>End Of The Ice Age</u>

Most scientists agree that there was a time (and maybe more than one) when the earth was covered with ice. Morris agreed that the earth has gone through an Ice Age.

> As evidence that the Ice Age constitutes a catastrophe that is utterly inexplicable in terms of present processes, one need only recall again the fact that there are dozens of hypotheses that have been advanced attempting to explain its cause and mechanism; all have had grave defects and none has yet been generally accepted.[26]

As he does with almost everything else that has happened to the earth, he presented the Flood as the cause of the Ice Age.

> However, it appears that the Flood events, and particularly the associated atmospheric changes, can once again suggest a cause adequate to explain this event also.[27]

Other YECs have taken this possibility and used it as if it has been proven true. I once was listening to the radio on a Saturday afternoon when I heard a YEC being interviewed about the Ice Age. He described just how it happened at the end of the flood when the water started receding. It was as if he had been an eye witness to it all! Dr. John Morris continues to promote this teaching with the articles he writes through the Institute of Creation Research.

> Rainfall continued its intensity, with swollen streams and violent storms. Calculations show that the ocean's heat would take at least 600 years or so to dissipate, and that during this period the "Ice Age" dominated.[28]

Maybe the reader can explain how the increased heat from the volcanoes could cause an Ice Age, but I cannot! It is just one more of their manufactured and totally unscientific teachings that they use to try to justify their theory.

I do have a possible explanation of how an Ice Age could have occurred. If the RTRs are correct that the earth had become without form and void and darkness covered the face of the deep, we have no way of knowing how long it was covered with that darkness. If the warmth from the sun's rays were not allowed to touch the earth for a long period of time, it is obvious that the earth could have gone through an Ice Age just prior to the six days work. It is interesting that Morris presented a quote from a book that he referenced that said the earth suddenly started warming up about 11,000 years ago.

> From the evidence listed above it is clear that a major fluctuation in climate occurred close to 11,000 years

ago. The primary observation that both surface ocean temperatures and deep sea sedimentation rates were abruptly altered at this time is supplemented by evidence from more local systems. The level of the Great Basin lakes fell from the highest terraces to a position close to that observed at present. The silt and clay load of the Mississippi river was suddenly retained in the alluvial valley and delta. A rapid ice retreat opened the northern drainage systems of the Great Lakes and terrestrial temperatures rose to nearly interglacial levels in Europe. In each case the transition is the most obvious feature of the entire record.[29]

Of course, Morris disagreed with the date of 11,000 years ago because it was about 7,000 years before the time of the flood. He ignored the fact that 11,000 years is just before the time he believes the six days work was done. This would validate the RTRs contention that an earth showing the results of destruction brought about by the judgment of God was transformed into a beautiful and inhabitable place about that point in time.

Use Of Radioactive Data

One issue that has caused the YECs much dismay is the use of radioactive data in determining the age of earth and the things on it. The most familiar one is the use of Carbon 14 dating. When an animal dies, the carbon that is in its system begins to decay at a certain rate and tests can be made on the remains to determine how long it has been dead. But, it is only useful if the item being studied is less than 65,000 years old because all the measurable carbon is gone by that time. Morris presented not only the results that have come from this test but from many other radioactive tests as well.

He presented the Lead Age Method, the Rubidium Method, the Potassium Method, and the significance of other radioactive data. They all present the age of the earth as being millions or billions of years old. He gave two reasons why all the results were wrong – the flood changed them or God created the earth with these things already appearing old.

He gave three reasons as to why he believed that Carbon 14 dating is wrong:[30]

1. The loss of the earth's canopy affected the carbon dioxide in the atmosphere,

2. The influx of carbon due to the volcanoes erupting during the flood,

3. There quite probably was a marked increase in the rate of formation of Carbon 14 atoms at the time of the Deluge due to the greater effectiveness of the cosmic radiation.

Since all the other methods of radioactive data all agree fairly close together, he surmises that maybe God created the earth with these things appearing old. After all, Adam was created full-grown and there were evidently full-grown trees in the garden that did not have growth rings.

> In the absence of specific revelation, it seems impossible to decide this question with finality. However, it is more satisfying teleologically, and therefore more reasonable, to infer that all these primeval clocks, since they were "wound up" at the same time, were also set to "read" the same time. Whatever this "setting" was, we may call it the "apparent age" of the earth, but the "true age" of the earth can only be known by means of divine revelation.[31]

Of course, to the YECs the true age of the earth can only be what they theorize it to be.

He admitted that the vast difference in the age calculated by the scientists and what he believed was hard to justify. He knew that even an error in the scientist's calculations would still not put the two ages close together.

> Even though experimental errors may be important, the measurements are still sufficiently accurate to give in most cases ages of at least the right order of magnitude. For example, a measurement indicating an age, say of one billion years, could hardly be in error by more than a factor of 10, and this would still give a hundred million years, nothing remotely comparable to the few thousand years implied by the Bible. Furthermore, it will be maintained that even though any given age measurement may be completely erroneous due to leaching or emanation or some other effect, there are many cases now known where the age estimate has been checked by two or more different methods, independently.[32]

Once again, his problem is not with what the scientists have discovered, but how he interprets the Bible. To the RTRs, it doesn't matter what happened billions of years ago because our eternal God was there to do it.

Age of Dinosaurs

The one part of creation that seems to fascinate people the most is the dinosaur.

It is so different from any of the other animals that we have on earth today. Scientists have their beliefs from the skeletons that have been found and the YECs have their belief on why dinosaurs are not here today.

According to scientific discoveries, scientists believe:

> The dinosaurs first appeared on earth nearly 250 million years ago in a time period known as Triassic. They grew in numbers during the Jurassic time period and dominated earth during the Cretaceous time period. They lived on earth for nearly 200 million years – 40,000 times as long as recorded human history. But, then suddenly they all mysteriously disappeared at the end of the Cretaceous Period about 65 million years ago.[33]

These dates may vary somewhat from other sources but they are fairly consistent. Some believe that an asteroid hit the earth causing their extinction.

The YECs believe that the dinosaurs were created at the same time as Adam and all the other creatures in Genesis 1. I have heard many YECs give explanations on why they believe the dinosaur became extinct. Some claim that they were too big to go on the ark, yet God told Noah to take two of every animal. Some said Noah only took little baby dinosaurs on the ark and they were unable to survive due to all the changes made on the earth by the flood. I don't believe God allowed any of the species that were on the ark to die before they had reproduced after their own kind. I heard Kent Hovind (a YEC) of Creation Science Evangelism at one of his speaking engagements say that he believed there were still dinosaurs on earth today.

There is quite a difference in believing the last dinosaur existed 65 million years ago and believing the first existed only 6,000 years ago! The scientists have formed their belief based on their studies of the skeletons found. As mentioned previously, Carbon 14 remains in bones for 65,000 years after the death of the animal. No carbon has ever been found in the bones of a dinosaur! The YECs have based their belief on their theory of all things being created 6,000 years ago.

I am not concerned about the age or period of the dinosaurs. Whenever they came into existence, God is the One who created them. Whenever they became extinct, God had a hand in that also. God was in control then as He is now and always will be!

Prehistoric Man

One of the most difficult things for some people to accept is the belief about prehistoric man. We have often made assumptions about things we believe without really having a reason to believe those things. Most people have just assumed that there is some relationship between prehistoric man and those of us who live today.

When God created Adam and placed him in the Garden of Eden, he was superior to anything that we can imagine. In Genesis 4, we are introduced to Adam's grandchildren and they were building cities, working with metals, farming, ranching, and playing music. It wasn't many centuries until man would be building great pyramids and other structures that amaze even modern man with all his technology. Man has not evolved but rather devolved from the great first man that God created! When you see a picture of an ape-looking man walking around stooped over with a club in his hand, he is not a descendant of Adam, nor is he a forefather of Adam.

Scientists have discovered the remains of many man-like species that once roamed the earth. There were differences in their appearances in different periods of time. It was once believed that each one of the species evolved from the previous one, but DNA tests and other discoveries have proven that theory to be false.

> Fossilized bones were found in 2000. The complete skull of Homo erectus was found within walking distance of an upper jaw of Homo habilis, and both dated from the same general time period. That makes it unlikely that Homo erectus evolved from Homo habilis, researchers said. The two species lived near each other, but probably didn't interact, each having its own "ecological niche." Homo habilis was likely more vegetarian while Homo erectus ate some meat.[34]

It was believed that modern man descended from Neanderthals or Cro-Magnon man, but recent tests have proved that to be incorrect also. It was reported in Discovery Health News on November 15, 2006, that DNA tests made on a 38,000 year old male Neanderthal uncovered in Vindija, Croatia, proved that modern man could not have descended from him.[35]

For many years, scientists have been searching for the 'missing link' between prehistoric man and modern man. It will never be found because there is no link. Every thing that lived prior to the earth having become without form and void died leaving a dead planet. God then created Adam to be the father of a new species on a renovated earth. Only descendants of

Adam can properly be called 'man'. Those who existed prior to that are only man-like to us.

Some may wonder if the pre-historic species will be in heaven. I have my views on this. When the angels were created, no provision was made for them to ever be redeemed if they sinned against God. When Lucifer sinned and was cast down, he had to remain in that fallen state. The same is true for his angels that followed him.

When God created Adam, He made him in His own image. Being made in the image of God involves much more than we have ever understood. It did mean that man would be a triune being – body, soul, and spirit. God is also triune – Father, Son, and Holy Spirit. Man could have originally had a garment of light about him that made him distinct from all other creatures, similar to the garment of light in which God is clothed (Psalm 104:2). When Adam and Eve sinned, I believe the light went out and they saw they that were naked, and were then ashamed. Adam and Eve were also created to dwell somewhere forever since they each had an eternal soul. All of these things were included in them being created in the image of God. Therefore, when Adam and Eve sinned, God offered a redemption that would restore them to a condition where they could dwell with Him forever. God offered this provision to no other created being. Those who refuse His offer of salvation will still exist forever, but, unfortunately, it will not be with Him!

The angels that kept their first estate will remain in that state and dwell with the Lord forever. The only other creatures that have that privilege are the descendants of Adam who accept the offer of redemption that God has provided. It may be against all that we have previously assumed, but prehistoric beings that have the appearance of man were created by God, but evidently not in His image. I do not believe they had eternal souls to live forever. What God did in creating Adam was something He had never done before!

༄

I have tried to present some of the scientific evidence that has been discovered on earth that reveals much about its history. Much was taken from the book *"The Genesis Flood"* written by Henry Morris. Most YECs use his explanations to justify their beliefs that all things were created just a few thousand years ago. I have tried to show that most of the scientific reasons they have for what they believe are not accurate or reliable. Much more information included in Morris' book that is also based on hypotheses and conjecture could have been presented, but space would not allow it. I want you to know that I am not alone in what I believe about the so-called science espoused by the YECs.

Whitcomb and Morris asked Dr. John C. McCampbell, Professor & Head of the Department of Geology at the University of Southwestern Louisiana to write the Foreword to *The Genesis Flood*. It was evident that he believed that God is the Creator and the biblical account of creation is accurate. He did not agree with their interpretations, however, as he stated in the following paragraph.

From the writer's viewpoint, as a professional geologist, these explanations and contentions are difficult to accept. For the present at least, although quite ready to recognize the inadequacies of Lyellian uniformitarianism, I would prefer to hope that some other means of harmonization of religion and geology, which retains the essential structure of modern historical geology, could be found.[36]

The term 'Lyellian uniformitarianism' is a term that is used to describe the belief that everything happening at the present has also always happened in the past. If this were true, then all the evidence found on earth would have been generated by conditions very similar to what we have today. It is obvious from his writings, that he did not accept that theory, but neither did he accept the writings of the authors for whom he was writing the Foreword. It is quite astounding that he would be asked to write their Foreword when he did not even agree with their geological explanations!

I want to again state the principle that the validity of a group's beliefs is most often determined by the validity of the evidence they use to reach their conclusions. The inadequacy of the evidence used by the YECs has been revealed. They had to contrive and generate possibilities that could somehow explain the old appearance of a young earth to allow their theory to be accepted.

Dr. McCampbell wanted the harmonization of religion and geology. The RTRs have it. Their interpretation of the work of creation presents an old earth with many signs of what happened a very long time ago, and a recent reconstruction of the earth and the creation of new creatures to dwell on it. The geologists have never discovered anything to contradict this theory! What the earth has to say agrees exactly with what the RTRs are teaching.

Some may think that what one believes and teaches about creation is not important. I totally disagree! The propagation of the gospel of Jesus Christ is by far the most important message that we should be sharing. But, what we believe and teach about other matters can determine whether sinners have enough confidence in us to accept the truth about Jesus Christ as we share the gospel with them.

If a true scientist is lost and reads the scientific teachings of the YECs he would see so many things that he knows are totally false that he would have doubts about anything else they teach, even if it is as true as the gospel. Our young people who grow up being taught the science of the YECs and then study true science themselves will become so disillusioned that they could begin to wonder if all they have been taught about Jesus is true. The primary responsibility of every Christian is to share the gospel with others, so we cannot afford to let anything else in our lives or in our other teachings cause them to doubt our message. The Apostle Paul was dealing with this very matter when he wrote, *"Let not then your good be evil spoken of"* (Romans 14:16).

The lesson is clear. The earth has a lot to say. When it is accurately heard, it will agree with what the Bible has to say if it is accurately interpreted!

Chapter 4
THE CREATOR OF CHAOS

As we have already discovered there are many fascinating topics of study found in the Bible. The reality of creation, heaven and hell, etc., are only some of the things revealed in the Bible that we would love to know more about. Enough information is given, however, to cause us to rejoice in what is revealed. Another revelation that is equally fascinating is the reality and work of angels. While we are given a lot of information concerning them, we want to know more. It is quite amazing that one of those marvelous created beings would become the creator of all the chaos affecting our world today!

The Bible doesn't reveal the exact number of the angels. We are only told that they are too many to be counted, or perhaps God just didn't want us to know the number. *"But ye are come unto mount Sion, and unto the city of the living God, the heavenly Jerusalem, and to an innumerable company of angels"* (Hebrews 12:22). We do know God created each of them since they evidently do not have reproductive organs and are unable to bring forth after their own kind. The bodies of glorified saints were compared to the bodies of angels: *"For when they shall rise from the dead, they neither marry, nor are given in marriage; but are as the angels which are in heaven"* (Mark 12:25). When God was speaking to Satan about his condition before his sin, He made the following statement, *"Thou wast perfect in thy ways from the day that thou wast created, till iniquity was found in thee"* (Ezekiel 28:15).

We are given some information about the ministry of angels. The Bible describes them as special ministers from God to every person who accepts Jesus as Savior. *"Are they not all ministering spirits, sent forth to minister for them who shall be heirs of salvation?"* (Hebrews 1:14). This verse seems to teach that every Christian has a guardian angel. It may very well be true. We would all be very surprised if we knew what the angels do for us every day! Even little children who have not yet come to the age of accountability have angels watching over them. *"Take heed that ye despise not one of these little ones; for I say unto you, That in heaven their angels do always behold the face of my Father which is in heaven"* (Matthew 18:10).

Angels are invisible to the natural human eye but there have been occasions when it was necessary for them to become visible and God revealed their presence. When Elisha and his servant awoke one morning surrounded by a huge army, the servant was fearful. Elisha simply asked the Lord to open the servant's eyes to see who was there to protect them. *"And he answered, Fear not: for they that be with us are more than they that be with them. And Elisha prayed, and said, LORD, I pray thee, open his eyes, that he may see. And the LORD opened the eyes of the young man; and he saw: and, behold, the mountain was full of horses and chariots of fire round about Elisha"* (2 Kings 6:16, 17).

The night Peter was kept in prison in Jerusalem expecting to be killed the next day, he was awakened by an angel who led him outside the jail and then disappeared: *"And when Peter was come to himself, he said, Now I know of a surety, that the Lord hath sent his angel, and hath delivered me out of the hand of Herod, and from all the expectation of the people of the Jews"* (Acts 12:11). Angels also appeared to the women at the empty tomb (Luke 24:4) and to the disciples on the Mount of Olives after the Lord's ascension (Acts 1:10).

There also seems to be a rank among the angels. Two of these are seraphim and cherubim. When Isaiah saw the glory of the Lord in Isaiah 6, he said there were seraphim crying "Holy, holy, holy". The word seraphim is the plural word for 'seraph'. In many places, cherubim (plural of cherub) are seen ministering for the Lord. Cherubim were put at the gate of the garden to keep Adam and Eve from going back to the tree of life. From what is revealed in Scripture it certainly seems that the seraphim and cherubim were both placed in exalted positions by the Lord.

Another thing of interest concerning the angels is the fact that three of them are given names – Gabriel, Michael, and Lucifer (Satan). They are mentioned in different places in the Bible and there is a consistency in what each one is doing on every occasion.

Angels In The Ministry Of God

Gabriel appears to be the angel of intellect who was sent to share very important information. Tradition has caused many to believe that Gabriel's primary job is blowing a trumpet, however, the Bible doesn't mention him blowing a trumpet.

God was sending him to deliver a message each time his name is mentioned in Scripture. The sounding of a trumpet can signify the proclaiming of a message of glad tidings.

After Daniel saw the vision of the ram and he goat in Daniel 8:1-15, he was seeking an explanation of the vision when he suddenly heard a voice: *"And I heard a man's voice between the banks of Ulai, which called, and said, Gabriel, make this man to understand the vision"* (Daniel 8:16). Gabriel then appeared and gave him the meaning.

Later, when Daniel realized that the time of their captivity in Babylon was completed according to the prophecy of Jeremiah, he prayed one of the most beautiful and powerful prayers found in the Bible (Daniel 9:1-19). He was asking God about the future of the Jewish people, the city of Jerusalem, and the Temple. It was a prayer that Daniel never completed: *"Yea, whiles I was speaking in prayer, even the man Gabriel, whom I had seen in the vision at the beginning, being caused to fly swiftly, touched me about the time of the evening oblation. And he informed me, and talked with me, and said, O Daniel, I am now come forth to give thee skill and understanding"* (Daniel 9:21, 22). It was then that Gabriel gave Daniel the prophecy of the Seventy Weeks that is one of the most remarkable prophecies that any man has ever received.

Zacharias and Elizabeth were an elderly couple who had served God faithfully. For many years they had prayed that God would bless them with a child. They thought God had refused to answer their prayer, but He was only postponing His answer. When they were very old, an angel appeared with the news that Elizabeth would bear a son and call his name 'John'.

It was when Zacharias asked the angel why he should believe him that the angel identified himself: *"And the angel answering said unto him, I am Gabriel, that stand in the presence of God; and am sent to speak unto thee, and to show thee these glad tidings"* (Luke 1:19).

God used Gabriel to deliver some very precious messages, but He saved the best for the last time his name is found in the Bible: *"And in the sixth month the angel Gabriel was sent from God unto a city of Galilee, named Nazareth, To a virgin espoused to a man whose name was Joseph, of the house of David; and the virgin's name was Mary"* (Luke 1:26, 27). Gabriel delivered God's message to Mary that she would be the one who would bring God's Son into the world.

Michael seems to be the angel that is involved in spiritual warfare. Each time his name is mentioned he is involved in some kind of conflict. In particular, he is identified as a special prince for the Jewish people.

In Daniel 10, Daniel had a vision by the side of the river Hiddekel. His description of the man he saw was so similar to John's vision of Jesus on the Isle of Patmos that he certainly must have seen the pre-incarnate Christ! He prayed for an explanation and an angel finally appeared. While the angel did not identify himself, he very well could have been Gabriel since he came with a special message from God. What is of special interest is that he had tried to come three weeks earlier but had been hindered by the prince of Persia. The prince of Persia may be a reference to Satan. Regardless, what happened to the angel is very significant: *"But the prince of the kingdom of Persia withstood me one and twenty days: but, lo, Michael, one of the chief princes, came to help me"* (Daniel 10:13). At the end of his meeting with Daniel, he gave the final information: *"But I will show thee that which is noted in the scripture of truth: and there is none that holdeth with me in these things, but Michael your prince"* (Daniel 10:21). You will note that Michael is called 'one of the chief princes' and 'your prince'.

Daniel presented a picture of the Great Tribulation as he opened the last chapter of his book and revealed the work of Michael: *"And at that time shall Michael stand up, the great prince which standeth for the children of thy people: and there shall be a time of trouble, such as never was since there was a nation even to that same time: and at that time thy people shall be delivered, every one that shall be found written in the book"* (Daniel 12:1). Here he is identified as the great prince that stands for the children of Daniel's people (the Jews).

God would not allow Moses to enter the Promised Land because he smote the rock the second time after being told to only speak to it (Numbers 20:7-12). Therefore, before Joshua took command over the people to lead them in, God took Moses up on a mountain and there took his life and apparently buried him. No one knows the exact location, but the New Testament tells us about an event that took place: *"Yet Michael the archangel, when contending with the devil he disputed about the body of Moses, durst not bring against him a railing accusation, but said, The Lord rebuke thee"* (Jude 9). We can only imagine what Satan would have done if he could have had the body! He could have used it to build a monument to be an object of worship to turn people from God. Regardless, it was Michael that God used to overcome Satan in the conflict. Michael was called 'the archangel' meaning 'the strong angel' as if there is only one who holds that title.

It was also Michael who was used to cast Satan and his angels out of heaven: *"And there was war in heaven: Michael and his angels fought against the dragon; and the dragon fought and his angels"* (Revelation 12:7). This is another incident about which we would love to have more information, but our curiosity must wait.

Lucifer is the other angel who is identified by name. This was his name before his rebellion against God. Consequently, he is no longer referred to as Lucifer, but is called Satan, devil, dragon, serpent, and many other names. What happened as a result of his rebellion is described in the following verses, *"And there appeared another wonder in heaven; and behold a great red dragon, having seven heads and ten horns, and seven crowns upon his heads. And his tail drew the third part of the stars of heaven, and did cast them to the earth — And the great dragon was cast out, that old serpent, called the Devil, and Satan, which deceiveth the whole world: he was cast out into the earth, and his angels were cast out with him"* (Revelation 12:3,4a, 9). The term 'stars of heaven' is believed to be a reference to the angels who followed him in his rebellion since an angel is called a 'star' in Revelation 9:1. The fact that he was cast down to the earth, however, is very significant.

The particular area of Lucifer's original work is not as easy to identify as that of Gabriel and Michael. One thing that stands out repeatedly, however, is his relationship with the earth. This will be revealed in the rest of this study and you will understand why it seems likely that he was over the physical creation.

It is very possible that the earth was like a sparkling diamond in all of creation and it was the center of his domain.

Since only three angels are called by name and one third of the angels fell with Satan causes some to assume that each of the named angels had one third under their authority. It may be a valid assumption.

The Rebellion And Fall Of Lucifer

There are two texts in the Bible that are generally accepted to be sources of information concerning Lucifer's sin. They are found in Isaiah and Ezekiel. Although Isaiah was prophesying against the king of Babylon and Ezekiel against the king of Tyrus, it is evident they were not referring to a mere human in their respective texts.

Isaiah is the prophet who called him Lucifer and presented the sin of his desire to be equal with God. Isaiah revealed the five 'I wills' of Lucifer against the will of God.

> *"How art thou fallen from heaven, O Lucifer, son of the morning! how art thou cut down to the ground, which didst weaken the nations! For thou hast said in thine heart, I will ascend into heaven, I will exalt my throne above the stars of God: I will sit also upon the mount of the congregation, in the sides of the north: I will ascend above the heights of the clouds; I will be like the most High. Yet thou shalt be brought down to hell, to the sides of the pit"* (Isaiah 14:12-15)

He must have been on earth when he made his rebellion since he desired to <u>ascend</u> into heaven above the heights of the clouds. It is very important to note also that he only wanted to be like the most High. He knew that nothing could be greater than God!

Ezekiel described the beauty and greatness of Lucifer and his dwelling place before sin took it all from him.

"Son of man, take up a lamentation upon the king of Tyrus, and say unto him, Thus saith the Lord GOD; Thou sealest up the sum, full of wisdom, and perfect in beauty. Thou hast been in Eden the garden of God; every precious stone was thy covering, the sardius, topaz, and the diamond, the beryl, the onyx, and the jasper, the sapphire, the emerald, and the carbuncle, and gold: the workmanship of thy tabrets and of thy pipes was prepared in thee in the day that thou wast created. Thou art the anointed cherub that covereth; and I have set thee so: thou wast upon the holy mountain of God; thou hast walked up and down in the midst of the stones of fire. Thou wast perfect in thy ways from the day that thou wast created, till iniquity was found in thee. By the multitude of thy merchandise they have filled the midst of thee with violence, and thou hast sinned: therefore I will cast thee as profane out of the mountain of God: and I will destroy thee, O covering cherub, from the midst of the stones of fire. Thine heart was lifted up because of thy beauty, thou hast corrupted thy wisdom by reason of thy brightness: I will cast thee to the ground, I will lay thee before kings, that they may behold thee. Thou hast defiled thy sanctuaries by the multitude of thine iniquities, by the iniquity of thy traffic; therefore will I bring forth a fire from the midst of thee, it shall devour thee, and I will bring thee to ashes upon the earth in the sight of all them that behold thee. All they that know thee among the people shall be astonished at thee:

thou shalt be a terror, and never shalt thou be any more"
(Ezekiel 28:12-19)

He was created with many precious stones covering him and even musical instruments were a part of his being. His earthly dwelling place was called Eden, the garden of God. I believe the description *"Thou sealest up the sum"* is stating that Lucifer was the very crown of that creation and he stood out above everything else. As a result of his sin, however, he was cast down to the ground (Ezekiel 28:17). The word 'ground' is the Hebrew word ERETS that is translated 'earth' in Genesis 1:1.

Jesus was an eyewitness to all that happened. When His disciples returned to Him and were amazed that devils were subject to them, He revealed that He saw the leader of all the devils when he was cast down: *"And he said unto them, I beheld Satan as lightning fall from heaven"* (Luke 10:18). Lucifer, the shining one, hit the earth like lightning with all of its destructive forces.

Satan Is Presented As A Prince

After his fall, Lucifer became the one we know as Satan, or devil. He was no longer in the position that he was created to fill, but the Bible still repeatedly calls him a prince. He is referred to as prince of devils, or Beelzebub. In other words, he is recognized as being over all the demon spirits that are on earth.

"But the Pharisees said, He casteth out devils through the prince of the devils" (Matthew 9:34)

"But when the Pharisees heard it, they said, This fellow doth not cast out devils, but by Beelzebub the prince of the devils" (Matthew 12:24)

"And the scribes which came down from Jerusalem said, He hath Beelzebub, and by the prince of the devils casteth he out devils" (Mark 3:22)

"But some of them said, He casteth out devils through Beelzebub the chief of the devils" (Luke 11:15)

While the people were talking about Jesus in each of these cases, they were accusing Him of being Satan.

Satan is also called the prince of this world or god of this world. This seems to infer that this earth is still part of his domain.

"Now is the judgment of this world: now shall the prince of this world be cast out" (John 12:31)

"Hereafter I will not talk much with you: for the prince of this world cometh, and hath nothing in me" (John 14:30)

"Of judgment, because the prince of this world is judged" (John 16:11)

"In whom the god of this world hath blinded the minds of them which believe not, lest the light of the glorious gospel of Christ, who is the image of God, should shine unto them" (2 Corinthians 4:4)

It was Jesus who called him the prince of this world and Paul through his inspired writing referred to him as the god of this world. Each of them used different Greek words which were translated 'world'. Jesus used the word KOSMOS which means beauty and arrangement and sometimes refers to mankind (John 3:16; Romans 5:12). Paul used the word AION which means age or dispensation (Galatians 1:4; Titus 2:12).

He is also called the prince of the power of the air and recognized as the one who is over all the wicked spiritual powers of the world.

> *"Wherein in time past ye walked according to the course of this world* (AION), *according to the prince of the power of the air, the spirit that now worketh in the children of disobedience"* (Ephesians 2:2)

> *"For we wrestle not against flesh and blood, but against principalities, against powers, against the rulers of the darkness of this world* (KOSMOS), *against spiritual wickedness in high places"* (Ephesians 6:12)

It is at the end of the Tribulation Period when the kingdoms that now belong to Satan will be claimed by the Lord. *"And the seventh angel sounded; and there were great voices in heaven, saying, The kingdoms of this world are become the kingdoms of our Lord, and of his Christ; and he shall reign for ever and ever"* (Revelation 11:15). Until that time, however, Satan is the prince and god of this world.

We are given a lot of information about Satan, but we are not told where he was during the work of the six days. After God had finished His work, He placed man in the Garden with specific instructions: *"And the LORD God took the man, and put him into the garden of Eden to dress it and to keep it"* (Genesis 2:15). The Hebrew word SHAMAR that is translated 'keep' is also translated as 'preserve' a number of times. Although Adam and Eve had not yet sinned, God knew that there was someone else present in the Garden who wanted to take everything from them. What He had provided for them could be lost if they were not diligent.

Eventually, Satan used a serpent to cause Eve to question the goodness of God: *"Now the serpent was more subtle than any beast of the field which the LORD God had made. And he said unto the woman, Yea, hath God said, Ye shall not eat of every tree of the garden?"* (Genesis 3:1). Satan never reminds us of the good things God has given, but he tries to draw our attention to what we do not have. Eve's temptation became a sin that was followed by Adam's sin. Suddenly, they had failed to keep and preserve the Garden as God had commanded.

It is evident that Satan was in the Garden, but where was he during the work of the six days? After each day's work, a statement was made that God saw what He had just completed was good, except for the second day! The following verses describe what happened on that day and you will notice the word 'good' is not found.

"And God said, Let there be a firmament in the midst of the waters, and let it divide the waters from the waters. And God made the firmament, and divided the waters which were under the firmament from the waters which were above the firmament: and it was so. And God called the firmament Heaven. And the evening and the morning were the second day" (Genesis 1:6-8)

Did God just forget to say that it was good? Of course not! There is a reason for everything that God said as well as everything He did not say! It was on that day that He made the atmosphere (air) that is above the earth that is described as the domain of Satan, the prince of the power of the air. Could it be that the presence of Satan in that air prevented God from calling it 'good'? It is a definite possibility!

It is true that when God had finished all the work of the six days He observed everything that He had made and called it 'very good' (Genesis 1:31). He was talking about the work of all the six days in that verse, but the fact that He chose not to say it when He finished the second day is significant. There is a reason (or reasons) for this omission!

Satan's Relationship To The Earth

Satan's relationship with God was eternally changed when he dared to try to become like God. From verses that have already been presented, it is obvious that he fell from heaven back to the earth. Yet, there are other verses that reveal that he can still leave earth from time to time to appear before God.

> *"Now there was a day when the sons of God came to present themselves before the LORD, and Satan came also among them. And the LORD said unto Satan, Whence comest thou? Then Satan answered the LORD, and said, From going to and fro in the earth, and from walking up and down in it"* (Job 1:6, 7)

> *"Again there was a day when the sons of God came to present themselves before the LORD, and Satan came also among them to present himself before the LORD. And the*

LORD said unto Satan, From whence comest thou? And Satan answered the LORD, and said, From going to and fro in the earth, and from walking up and down in it" (Job 2:1, 2)

If he was involved in this activity in Job's day, there is no reason to believe that he is not doing the same today. We are also told that when the Great Tribulation begins he will no longer be able to go before God, but will be consigned only to the earth.

"And I heard a loud voice saying in heaven, Now is come salvation, and strength, and the kingdom of our God, and the power of his Christ: for the accuser of our brethren is cast down, which accused them before our God day and night" (Revelation 12:10).

Satan was cast back to the earth when he first rebelled against God but will be limited to the earth at the very end. In Isaiah's account, he wrote *"how art thou cut down to the ground (ERETS)"* (Isaiah 14:12). Ezekiel referred to the earth twice, *"I will cast thee to the ground (ERETS)"* (Ezekiel 28:17) and *"I will bring thee to ashes upon the earth (ERETS)"* (Ezekiel 28:18). Isaiah was probably referring to what happened at the rebellion. Ezekiel could be speaking about the rebellion and the final casting down that will take place in the Great Tribulation when Satan will be confined to the earth.

When Jesus saw Satan falling as lightning from heaven, one would have to believe that He saw him falling to the earth (Luke 10:18) immediately after his rebellion. The following verses from Revelation seem to describe what happened at the beginning and what will be completed at the end.

"And his tail drew the third part of the stars of heaven, and did cast them to the earth" (Revelation 12:4)

"And the great dragon was cast out, that old serpent, called the Devil, and Satan, which deceiveth the whole world: he was cast out into the earth, and his angels were cast out with him" (Revelation 12:9)

"Therefore rejoice, ye heavens, and ye that dwell in them. Woe to the inhabiters of the earth and of the sea! for the devil is come down unto you, having great wrath, because he knoweth that he hath but a short time" (Revelation 12:12)

The first two verses more than likely describe the judgment at his rebellion while the last definitely reveals what will happen in the Tribulation period.

The fact that Satan's last acts of evil will be upon the earth should not be a surprise, since he was on earth when he planned his first rebellion against God. Isaiah reveals the plans of Lucifer in his rebellion: *"For thou hast said in thine heart, I will ascend into heaven, I will exalt my throne above the stars of God — I will ascend above the heights of the clouds"* (Isaiah 14:13, 14). As previously stated, he must have been on the earth to want to ascend up into heaven. In Exekiel we are told of him walking in Eden, the garden of God (which certainly seems to be on earth), prior to iniquity being found in him.

In the New Testament, there is a verse that is relevant concerning what happened to the angels who followed him.

"And the angels which kept not their first estate, but left their own habitation, he hath reserved in everlasting chains under darkness unto the judgment of the great day" (Jude 6)

You will notice from this verse that the angels had a 'first estate' that was the place of 'their own habitation'. They failed to keep it so they are now in everlasting chains. Their first estate was on earth and Lucifer was their ruler.

∽

In this chapter, I have tried to present evidence about the created beings that we know as angels. In particular, many verses concerning Lucifer (Satan) have been presented. The Scriptures give details about him prior to his sin, about his sin, and about his work and position after his sin. All the evidence proves that he was the first to sin against God and, thus, he became the creator of the chaos that first touched the earth.

The possibility has been presented in the previous chapters that God's judgment against Satan's rebellion may have gone on for a very long time, until the earth finally was without form and void. All former life had died and the earth was an uninhabitable planet. It was from that condition that God did the six days work and created man, fish, fowl, and other creatures to dwell on the newly renovated and perfect earth. But is there any biblical reason to believe that Lucifer's sin brought about the condition of the earth being *"without form and void"* as described in Genesis 1:2?

Note the stark similarities of the following statements:

"That made the world as a wilderness, and destroyed the cities thereof"

"The fruitful place was a wilderness, and all the cities thereof were broken down"

Do you believe that these two descriptions are talking about different events, or do you see the possibility that they are describing the same event? Note that each statement mentions the world becoming a wilderness and cities being destroyed.

The first statement is taken from Isaiah 14:17 and reveals what happened after the sin of Lucifer. The second is from Jeremiah 4:26 where he described a vision he was given.

"I beheld the earth, and, lo, it was without form, and void; and the heavens, and they had no light. I beheld the mountains, and, lo, they trembled, and all the hills moved lightly. I beheld, and, lo, there was no man, and all the birds of the heavens were fled. I beheld, and, lo, the fruitful place was a wilderness, and all the cities thereof were broken down at the presence of the LORD, and by his fierce anger" (Jeremiah 4:23-26)

As John was taken forward in time to see the vision of the last days in Revelation, Jeremiah was taken back in time to see what happened when the earth became without form and void. Through God's revelation, it was as if Jeremiah was actually present with God when the desolations occurred.

Jeremiah saw darkness covering the earth, mountains trembling, hills moving, and no living creatures left on earth as it was without form and void. It was then that he revealed that what was once a fruitful place had become a wilderness and all the cities were broken down. Jeremiah said it was all done *"at the presence of the Lord, and by his fierce anger"*. Isaiah stated the condition was a result of Lucifer's sin. If we allow the Bible to interpret itself, we will acknowledge that it is not only a possibility, but also a probability, that it was judgment from God because of the rebellion of Lucifer that resulted in the earth becoming without form and void.

In the very next verse, the Lord made a very special promise to Jeremiah: *"For thus hath the LORD said, The whole land shall be desolate; yet will I not make a full end"* (Jeremiah 4:27). The Hebrew word translated 'land' is the same ERETS that is translated 'earth' in Genesis 1:1, 2. Jeremiah was assured that God was not finished with the earth! Out of this condition of being without form and void He would do a wonderful work to restore the earth to a beautiful and inhabitable condition again. That is just what He did in the six days work when the earth went from ruin to restoration.

Everything on earth was affected by the curse brought about by Adam's sin. It is totally inconsistent to believe that our unchanging God would be so harsh in His judgment against Adam and not be just as harsh against the sin of Lucifer. Each of them was the crown of the creation over which they were placed and their sins would be equally judged.

If Adam's sin brought death to the animal kingdom that he had dominion over, it should be no surprise that Lucifer's sin would do the same to his domain. Because of Adam's sin, the earth is headed towards the great judgment of God that is called the Great Tribulation. Jesus said that all flesh will be destroyed unless He comes to bring that judgment to an end (Matthew 24:22). His coming will prevent the earth from once again becoming without form and void.

The next chapter will compare Lucifer and Adam as the crowns of their respective creations and how their sins brought destruction and death to their worlds.

Chapter 5
GOD'S JUDGMENT AGAINST REBELLION

God is not only the great Creator, but He is also the One who holds His creation together: *"For by him were all things created, that are in heaven, and that are in earth, visible and invisible, whether they be thrones, or dominions, or principalities, or powers: all things were created by him, and for him: And he is before all things, and by him all things consist"* (Colossians 1:16, 17). He has the power to cause all things to continue as created or He can bring judgment upon His creation that will totally change it. Our earth is different than it was when originally created and most of the changes are due to the judgments that have been brought about by God because of the rebellion that occurred against Him.

The biblical account of creation begins in the Bible's very first verse: *"In the beginning God created the heaven and the earth"* (Genesis 1:1). This verse only refers to the creation of the heaven and the earth, but I believe there were other creations near the beginning that are not mentioned in this verse.

The time when the angels were created is not given to us. We are told in Scripture that Lucifer was created (Ezekiel

28:15), and this would cause us to believe that all other angels were created as well, though the time of their creation is uncertain. It is my belief that they were created between the creation of the heaven and the creation of the earth in Genesis 1:1.

God reminded Job that He laid the foundations and the cornerstone of the earth, and He gave the response of the angels when they first viewed the newly created earth: *"When the morning stars sang together, and all the sons of God shouted for joy"* (Job 38:7). The angels (called morning stars and sons of God) had seen the stars, the sun, and other planets, but when they saw the earth they were overcome with singing and praising God for His latest work! The pictures of earth we have seen that were taken from space reveals that it is unique in its beauty. We certainly can understand the response of the angels. The important thing, however, is that this proves that the angels were created prior to the earth.

The beauty of the newly created earth must have been very meaningful to Lucifer since this would be the place of his domain. I believe that after the creation of the earth, God began to create creatures that would live on it. The fossil records that have been discovered prove that different creatures lived on earth at various ages. Lucifer would have also reigned over them as he enjoyed the work that God had provided for him. By the sovereign will of God, the judgment that began when Lucifer rebelled against God would not only affect the earth, but all the creatures that dwelt on it as well.

The fossil remains that are found in sedimentary rocks and other strata prove that living beings were on earth a very long time ago. The fossil remains of different kinds of creatures have been discovered in successive layers of rock revealing that God may have performed many creative acts in the early days of the earth. As an example, the dinosaurs suddenly appeared on earth about 250 million years ago and just as mysteriously, they vanished about 65 million years ago.

Every being that has ever lived on earth, whether it was a fish, fowl, tiny creature, or a very huge animal, were each from a species created by God. He is the source of all life! He is also the reason that many creatures became extinct. Geological discoveries reveal that prior to the earth becoming without form and void, God had created many creatures, and then many of them were destroyed by the judgments that He brought upon the earth.

The last judgment that God brought prior to the six days work resulted in the earth becoming without form and void with darkness covering the face of the deep. In that condition, light and warmth would be prevented from touching the surface of the earth, and it could easily have then become covered by a thick layer of ice. This condition would not only kill all creatures living on land, but would also kill all the fish living in the sea. No living creature would be left on earth after a period of time. The seeds and roots of plants could have been frozen and preserved to live again once warmth touched the face of the earth. This was the condition of the earth as described in Genesis 1:2.

The renovation of the earth's surface and the creation of new fish, fowl, animals, and man are presented in Genesis 1:3-27. Although the devil was still on the earth, God created Adam and gave him the responsibility of assuming authority over all of His new and renovated creation. Unfortunately, Adam and Eve also sinned and brought judgment on the creation that God had given them.

The sin of Lucifer brought the judgment of God on the original earth. When Adam and Eve sinned, the righteousness of God caused Him to place a curse on the newly renovated earth as well (Genesis 3:14-19). The lesson is very clear – any being that sins against God will be judged and His judgment will affect much more than just the guilty: *"But he that doeth wrong shall receive for the wrong which he hath done: and there is no respect of persons"* (Colossians 3:25). In their own respective times, Lucifer and Adam were both given dominion. However, their sins ultimately spoiled everything that was under them.

The Crowns of the Creations

After the original creation of the earth, Lucifer was the greatest of all the beings that dwelt on earth. The statement that God made to him through the prophet Ezekiel seems to verify his standing in that world.

"Son of man, take up a lamentation upon the king of Tyrus, and say unto him, Thus saith the Lord GOD; Thou sealest up the sum, full of wisdom, and perfect in beauty. Thou hast been in Eden the garden of God; every precious stone was thy covering, the sardius, topaz, and the diamond, the beryl, the onyx, and the jasper, the sapphire, the emerald, and the carbuncle, and gold: the workmanship of thy tabrets and of thy pipes was prepared in thee in the day that thou wast created. Thou art the anointed cherub that covereth; and I have set thee so: thou wast upon the holy mountain of God; thou hast walked up and down in the midst of the stones of fire. Thou wast perfect in thy

ways from the day that thou wast created, till iniquity was found in thee" (Ezekiel 28:12-15)

Since he 'sealed up the sum', it is difficult to imagine any creature being greater or outshining him.

We know that Adam was created to be the greatest in his world at the conclusion of the six days work.

"And God said, Let us make man in our image, after our likeness: and let them have dominion over the fish of the sea, and over the fowl of the air, and over the cattle, and over all the earth, and over every creeping thing that creepeth upon the earth. So God created man in his own image, in the image of God created he him; male and female created he them" (Genesis 1:26, 27)

In their newly created condition, all the creatures on earth must have been outstanding as they appeared, but Adam clearly was different and above them all!

It is expressly stated that man was made in the very image of God. This could imply that man was to be a triune being of body, soul and spirit as God exists in the three Persons of Father, Son, and Holy Spirit. It also means that man was a being who would have a never-ending soul and would always exist somewhere. Obviously, man was the only being created with a God consciousness and would be the only one who could live in fellowship with his Creator. But to really understand what it is to be created in the image of God, we must know something about His image.

No one knows what God looks like, but His appearance always seems to involve a bright light. The glory of God was seen as He revealed Himself to men at various times. The

Psalmist acknowledged that He wore light as a garment: *"Who coverest thyself with light as with a garment"* (Psalm 104:2). The Bible describes His brightness being observed by many and the Jews called it the 'Shekinah' glory of God.

When Moses came down from the mountain after spending time in the presence of the holy God, his face had absorbed some of that brightness: *"And the children of Israel saw the face of Moses, that the skin of Moses' face shone: and Moses put the veil upon his face again, until he went in to speak with him"* (Exodus 34:35).

After Daniel had been praying on the bank of the river, he was allowed to see a vision of the Lord. He described the brightness, *"His body also was like the beryl, and his face as the appearance of lightning, and his eyes as lamps of fire"* (Daniel 10:6).

The Apostle John was exiled on the Isle of Patmos when the Lord appeared to give him the Revelation. As John described the One he saw, it was very similar to what Daniel had seen, *"His countenance was as the sun shineth in his strength"* (Revelation 1:16). The fact that Jesus would appear in brightness would be no surprise to John since he had described the 'Light' in his previous books.

As he opened the Gospel of John, he presented Jesus as being God and the One who had made all things. Then, he introduced Him as the Light.

> *"In him was life; and the life was the light of men. And the light shineth in darkness; and the darkness comprehended it not. There was a man sent from God, whose name was John. The same came for a witness, to bear wit-*

ness of the Light, that all men through him might believe. He was not that Light, but was sent to bear witness of that Light. That was the true Light, which lighteth every man that cometh into the world" (John 1:4-9)

In his first Epistle he also described the Light: *"This then is the message which we have heard of him, and declare unto you, that God is light, and in him is no darkness at all"* (1 John 1:5). Twice in the Gospel of John, Jesus is quoted as saying, *"I am the light of the world"* (John 8:12, 9:5).

Saul of Tarsus was on the way to Damascus when the light from the Lord's presence appeared to him. The Lord could have made His appearance at any time, but He chose noon when the sunlight would be the brightest. Even in that brightness, however, the light from the Lord was obvious to all who were present: *"And it came to pass, that, as I made my journey, and was come nigh unto Damascus about noon, suddenly there shone from heaven a great light round about me"* (Acts 22:6). Paul went on to state that everyone present saw the light but did not hear the voice that spoke to him.

Many who have had a near death experience have described the bright light that they saw at the time. It seems evident that a bright light is associated with God. It should also be evident that the crowns of His creations would be over all the rest of their respective creations, but would each have some appearance of their Creator. That seems to be the case with both Lucifer and Adam.

Lucifer was given his name because of his brightness. The name 'Lucifer' means 'light bearer' or 'shining one'. All the angels evidently had some brightness associated with them since God called them 'morning stars' when He spoke to Job about them: *"When the morning stars sang together"* (Job 38:7). The morning star is considered to be one of the brightest stars or planets. The Psalmist stated that God had made the angels to be a flaming fire: *"Who maketh his angels spirits; his ministers a flaming fire"* (Psalm 104:4). Jesus described the fall of Lucifer back to earth as an appearance of lightning. Thus, those who saw Lucifer in the brilliance of his original appearance would have seen his likeness to his Creator.

One of the characteristics about Adam that was a result of being made in the image of God could be that he, too, was covered in a garment of light. When Adam and Eve sinned they saw that they were naked. What covered their nakedness before their sin? If it was a garment of light, then Eve's light went out the moment she sinned. That may explain the statement made by God through the Apostle Paul: *"For Adam was first formed, then Eve. And Adam was not deceived, but the woman being deceived was in the transgression"* (1 Timothy 2:13, 14). Adam was not deceived because he knew what had already happened to Eve as a result of her sin.

Adam faced a dilemma. He knew that if he took of the fruit as Eve had done then his light would also go out and death would ultimately come. But, if he did not take of the fruit, his light would remain and he would live, but he would have to live alone for eternity. Paul said that Adam was not deceived so he must have made a conscious decision knowing what the consequences would be.

If it is correct that Adam was clothed in a garment of light similar to Lucifer's original condition, the crowns of their respective creations both resembled their Creator as they reflected His brightness.

A Comparison of the Crowns of God's Creation

It is an interesting study to compare the similarities and differences between Lucifer and Adam, the crowns of God's creations. There are some things they share, yet there are other things about them that are totally different.

Lucifer was a created being, as were all the angels that followed him in his rebellion. Each of the fallen angels made the decision to follow Lucifer. Adam and Eve were the only created humans and all others descended from them through natural reproduction. When Adam and Eve, sinned they passed their depraved nature on to all their descendants: *"Wherefore, as by one man sin entered into the world, and death by sin; and so death passed upon all men, for that all have sinned"* (Romans 5:12).

Lucifer and Adam were both created to exist forever. When Lucifer entered into his rebellion there was no means of redemption provided for him. He will have to live forever in that sinful state of being out of favor with God. On the other hand, before the foundation of the world, God had made provision for a possible redemption for Adam should he become guilty of sin.

> *"For as much as ye know that ye were not redeemed with corruptible things, as silver and gold, from your vain conversation received by tradition from your fathers; But with the precious blood of Christ, as of a lamb without blemish and without spot: Who verily was foreordained before the foundation of the world, but was manifest in these last times for you"* (1 Peter 1:18-20)

Thus, Lucifer can never be reconciled to God. Conversely, the entire human race has been included in God's offer of reconciliation through the blood of Jesus Christ.

Adam was created as a triune being with body, soul and spirit: *"And the LORD God formed man of the dust of the ground* (BODY), *and breathed into his nostrils the breath of life* (SPIRIT); *and man became a living soul* (SOUL)"* (Genesis 2:7) (Emphasis mine). The body is of the earth and relates to the earth. The soul is the seat of personality that contains intellect, emotions and will and relates to other living beings. The spirit is the part of man that relates to God and allows fellowship with Him.

When a person dies, the body remains on the earth and returns to dust and ashes. The soul and spirit, however, will either go to hell or to heaven depending on whether or not the individual has received God's great salvation.

The person of Lucifer is not so easily understood. It is obvious that he is a real being with intellect, emotions, and will so he must have a personality. How that relates to a soul is not so clear. The Bible does seem to give an explanation for the bodies and spirits of the angels that followed him.

There are two verses in Scripture that reveal to us that the bodies of the fallen angels are kept in chains waiting for the judgment they will eventually face.

> *"For if God spared not the angels that sinned, but cast them down to hell* (TARTAROO), *and delivered them into chains of darkness, to be reserved unto judgment"* (2 Peter 2:4) (Emphasis mine)

"And the angels which kept not their first estate, but left their own habitation, he hath reserved in everlasting chains under darkness unto the judgment of the great day" (Jude 6)

The term for 'hell' that was used by Peter is TARTAROO. Since this is the only place the word is found in the Bible, we have no more information about the place to which this word refers. It seems evident that it is not the hell that contains the souls and spirits of the lost who have died. The Greek word that is used in the New Testament for that place is HADES. What both texts mentioned, however, is the fact that they are bound by chains and will remain so until they face the judgment of God.

Satan has disembodied spirits that are currently serving him on earth. The Bible refers to them as demons or devils. They do not have bodies to use (since their own angelic bodies are bound in chains) so they inhabit other bodies. When Jesus was about to drive the devils out of the body of the maniac of Gadara, the demons who possessed him requested to enter into a herd of swine.

"And he asked him, What is thy name? And he answered, saying, My name is Legion: for we are many. And he besought him much that he would not send them away out of the country. Now there was there nigh unto the mountains a great herd of swine feeding. And all the devils besought him, saying, Send us into the swine, that we may enter into them" (Mark 5:9-12).

Jesus also gave some general information about the unclean spirits that inhabit people and how they consider the human body as their home.

> *"When the unclean spirit is gone out of a man, he* (the unclean spirit) *walketh through dry places, seeking rest; and finding none, he saith, I will return unto my house* (the body of the man) *whence I came out. And when he cometh, he findeth it swept and garnished. Then goeth he, and taketh to him seven other spirits more wicked than himself; and they enter in, and dwell there: and the last state of that man is worse than the first"* (Luke 11:24-26) (Emphasis mine)

These unclean demon spirits that were on earth in the days of Jesus are still here and can still inhabit the bodies of animals and humans.

They know that they will eventually face the judgment of God. Matthew revealed this in the account he gave of the man from Gadara mentioned above: *"And, behold, they cried out, saying, What have we to do with thee, Jesus, thou Son of God? art thou come hither to torment us before the time?"* (Matthew 8:29). They knew they would face judgment, but they knew it was not yet time for that judgment. Therefore, they asked why Jesus had come to torment them 'before the time'.

While the respective bodies given to Lucifer and Adam were quite different, they were each allowed to live in a special garden that was created for them. Ezekiel referred to Lucifer's garden which was on earth prior to Genesis 1:2: *"Thou hast been in Eden the garden of God"* (Ezekiel 28:13). Likewise, God placed Adam in the Garden of Eden: *"And the LORD God took the man, and put him into the garden of Eden to dress it and to keep it"* (Genesis 2:15). The names were similar, but the descriptions given of each of the gardens were different. Both were beautiful places, however, and exactly what Lucifer and Adam would need for their respective lives.

Lucifer and Adam not only were given a special home in a garden, but each of them was given dominion over the earth on which they dwelt. The Bible specifically states that God gave Adam dominion over the earth and all the creatures that dwelt on it: *"Let them have dominion over the fish of the sea, and over the fowl of the air, and over the cattle, and over all the earth, and over every creeping thing that creepeth upon the earth"* (Genesis 1:26). It seems likely that Lucifer had previously been given dominion over his earth as well.

Satan made an interesting statement when he was tempting Jesus in the wilderness. In his efforts to try to get Jesus to worship him, he showed Him all the kingdoms of the world: *"And the devil said unto him, All this power will I give thee, and the glory of them: for that is delivered unto me; and to whomsoever I will I give it"* (Luke 4:6). You will notice that Satan said the kingdoms of the world had been delivered to him. Now, some say that they were not Satan's to offer, but if they were not then Jesus would not have been tempted! Since they had been delivered to him, one must wonder when the delivery was made. It must have been in the very beginning before his sin caused his possession to become without form and void.

Jesus did not correct the devil's claim of owning the kingdoms, but He told Satan to get behind Him, because He was only going to worship God. Satan is a liar and we know he would not have given the kingdoms of the world to Jesus, but they were and are his. The kingdoms of this world will become the kingdoms of Jesus when He comes to claim them for His own: *"And the seventh angel sounded; and there were great voices in heaven, saying, The kingdoms of this world are become the kingdoms of our Lord, and of his Christ; and he shall reign for ever and ever"* (Revelation 11:15). They will not become His because they are given to Him, but because He purchased all things for Himself!

Since Adam and Lucifer both had dominion over their respective worlds, it should be obvious that each of their sins would drastically affect everything in the kingdoms that were under them. Isaiah tells us about how the world was affected following Lucifer's sin: *"That made the world as a wilderness, and destroyed the cities thereof; that opened not the house of his prisoners"* (Isaiah 14:17). The Lord gave much more information about what happened to Adam's dominion after he and Eve had sinned.

> *"And the LORD God said unto the serpent, Because thou hast done this, thou art cursed above all cattle, and above every beast of the field; upon thy belly shalt thou go, and dust shalt thou eat all the days of thy life: And I will put enmity between thee and the woman, and between thy seed and her seed; it shall bruise thy head, and thou shalt bruise his heel. Unto the woman he said, I will greatly multiply thy sorrow and thy conception; in sorrow thou shalt bring forth children; and thy desire shall be to thy husband, and he shall rule over thee. And unto Adam he said, Because thou hast hearkened unto the voice of thy wife, and hast eaten of the tree, of which I commanded*

thee, saying, Thou shalt not eat of it: cursed is the ground for thy sake; in sorrow shalt thou eat of it all the days of thy life; Thorns also and thistles shall it bring forth to thee; and thou shalt eat the herb of the field; In the sweat of thy face shalt thou eat bread, till thou return unto the ground; for out of it wast thou taken: for dust thou art, and unto dust shalt thou return" (Genesis 3:14-19)

Every living creature was affected by the curse. The serpent was cursed above all the other beasts, but all were cursed. For Eve, child bearing would now involve great pain and she would be submissive to her husband. For Adam, the ground would no longer bring forth his fruit with little effort on his part. Even the ground was cursed to bring forth thorns and thistles.

The ultimate judgment would be that both Adam and Eve would die physically, and their bodies would return to the earth from whence they came. Of course, all the other living creatures upon earth would have to die as well.

The results of Lucifer's sin led to the earth becoming without form and void. The sin of Adam and Eve has left a tremendous curse on the earth thus far, but God is not finished, and His greatest judgments are yet to come.

The Rebellion of the Crowns of Creation

The rebellion of Lucifer with his five 'I wills' is presented in Isaiah 14:13, 14 with the final and ultimate sin being his desire to 'be like the most High'. It was his pride and arrogance that led to his desire to be a god.

In the account given by Ezekiel, he is obviously referring to Satan as he referenced his comments to the prince of Tyrus.

"Son of man, say unto the prince of Tyrus, Thus saith the Lord GOD; Because thine heart is lifted up, and thou hast said, I am a God, I sit in the seat of God, in the midst of the seas; yet thou art a man, and not God, though thou set thine heart as the heart of God — Wilt thou yet say before him that slayeth thee, I am God? but thou shalt be a man, and no God, in the hand of him that slayeth thee — Thine heart was lifted up because of thy beauty, thou hast corrupted thy wisdom by reason of thy brightness: I will cast thee to the ground, I will lay thee before kings, that they may behold thee" (Ezekiel 28:2, 9, 17)

Once again, the same sin is depicted as he allows his beauty and greatness to cause him to want to be like God.

Satan approached Eve through the serpent that was the most subtle of all the creatures in the garden. It was not the serpent, however, that caused Eve to sin. She saw that the forbidden tree was good for food, beautiful to look upon, and one to be desired for wisdom, but it wasn't a desire for the fruit of the tree that overcame her. Satan tempted her with the same thing that he was guilty of – the desire to be a god: *"For God doth know that in the day ye eat thereof, then your eyes shall be opened, and ye shall be as gods, knowing good and evil"* (Genesis 3:5).

Lucifer's desire to be like God brought many calamities against his world that resulted in the earth becoming without form and void in darkness. After Eve failed at becoming a god, she gave the fruit to her husband and he became guilty of sin. It would seem that their failures would cause everyone to realize the impossibility of becoming a god, but this is not the case at all! Satan still wants to be a god and is using man in an effort to accomplish his goal.

The last days of Adam's race upon earth will involve the coming of the Great Tribulation. It will be a time when God will pour out his wrath on an unbelieving world. A man who we know as the antichrist will come forth, who will be under the complete control of Satan and will be the personification of all that is evil. He will do everything he can to bring the earth under his control, even allowing the Jews to rebuild their Temple in Jerusalem at the beginning of that period.

In the middle of the Tribulation Period, he will eventually go into Jerusalem and sit in the Jewish Temple claiming that he is God and must be worshipped as such.

> *"Let no man deceive you by any means: for that day shall not come, except there come a falling away first, and that man of sin be revealed, the son of perdition; Who opposeth and exalteth himself above all that is called God, or that is worshipped; so that he as God sitteth in the temple of God, showing himself that he is God"* (2 Thessalonians 2:3, 4)

Satan has always wanted to have such a man since the Garden of Eden, but has been prohibited thus far. When Jesus returns to take all the saved away in the Rapture, however, the hindrance will be removed and that wicked person will be revealed.

> *"And then shall that Wicked be revealed, whom the Lord shall consume with the spirit of his mouth, and shall destroy with the brightness of his coming: Even him, whose coming is after the working of Satan with all power and signs and lying wonders"* (2 Thessalonians 2:8, 9)

The effort of the antichrist to control the earth under satanic control is revealed in Revelation 13 where he is identified as a beast. Another powerful being (commonly known as the false prophet) comes forth to promote the beast in his efforts to be recognized as God.

> *"And they worshipped the dragon which gave power unto the beast: and they worshipped the beast, saying, Who is like unto the beast? who is able to make war with him? — And I beheld another beast coming up out of the earth; and he had two horns like a lamb, and he spake as a dragon. And he exerciseth all the power of the first beast before him, and causeth the earth and them which dwell therein to worship the first beast, whose deadly wound was healed — Here is wisdom. Let him that hath understanding count the number of the beast: for it is the number of a man; and his number is Six hundred threescore and six"*
> (Revelation 13:4, 11, 12, 18)

This will be Satan's final effort to be God. The number 666 represents the satanic trinity. Satan is the false Father, the antichrist is the false Son, and the false prophet tries to be as the Holy Spirit. The number for the true trinity would be 777 with the number seven representing divine completeness.

The Great Tribulation will be concluded when Jesus comes in glory to bring it to an end. His first act will be to take the beast and false prophet and cast them both alive into the eternal lake of fire (Revelation 19:20). One thousand years later, Satan will join them (Revelation 20:10) and the final rebellion against God will be over. After all the efforts against Him, God will still be the one and only true God in the three Persons of the Father, Son, and Holy Spirit!

The Condemnation Against the Rebellion

After God created both Lucifer and Adam and gave them dominion over their respective worlds, each of them desired to leave their created positions in an effort to be equal with their Creator. The Scriptures clearly teach that in each case both offenders failed in their efforts and suffered the consequences of their sin. But, is that all that happened? Did God's judgment against them affect only them or were their places of dominion also touched by His judgment?

We know that God placed a curse upon Adam's world that would affect how he lived and ruled. It is difficult to imagine that the same God would not do the same to the world He had given to Lucifer after he had sinned. God is an unchanging God and one would suppose that He would react the same way with each of them. Our Bible gives many details about what happened in Adam's case because it is God's revelation to man. Although we are affected by the results of Lucifer's rebellion, our world is still under the curse placed upon it because of the sin of Adam and Eve. That curse is what causes most of our problems.

After the curse was placed on their respective worlds, Lucifer and Adam each had new difficulties in fulfilling his responsibilities. They had desired to be like Him, so God gave them the chance to see how they would function as a god in their respective worlds. They have been failures! What had been normal became abnormal, and neither could do anything to reverse the conditions. Every earthquake, volcano, drought, flood, hurricane, etc., has occurred because of the original sin of Lucifer, or because of Adam's sin in the Garden of Eden, and neither of them has been able to prevent the death and damage that has come.

The Scriptures tell us of cases where the judgment of God has fallen on certain generations because of the specific sins of the people who lived at a particular time. The best known is probably the flood of Noah's day, when God saw that every imagination of the thoughts of the people was evil continually (Genesis 6:5). God instructed Noah to build the ark that would become a place of salvation for the ones who would be spared from His judgment.

Some of the greatest judgments that have touched the earth, however, are the various catastrophes and calamities that have not only destroyed people, but have also changed planet earth. They are often called 'acts of God'. Some consider them as a normal part of our world, but they are certainly abnormal with respect to the original creation of the earth! Yet Satan and man can only suffer through the results because they are totally unable to stop them or stand against God when His will must be done.

Various geological formations reveal that planet earth went through many catastrophic events over a very long period of time. Most of them occurred prior to man being placed on earth in the six days work, so they must have happened as a direct result of the rebellion of Lucifer. Many other changes have occurred to the earth since the six days work because of God's judgment against Adam's sin. The greatest changes that will occur to earth as a consequence of man's sin, however, are yet to come.

After all the saved are caught up to meet the Lord in the air at the Rapture, God will begin to pour His wrath out upon the earth and the inhabitants left on it. It is the time previously identified as the Great Tribulation. It will be the greatest and most fierce judgment resulting from Adam's original sin and the failures of his descendants. Additionally, the earth will also be judged for how Jesus was treated when He came to earth. This Great Tribulation period will last for a total of seven years but the last 3 ½ years will be by far the most devastating.

There are many prophecies that describe the events of the Great Tribulation, and the period as described in Revelations surely lives up to its name! It will be a terrible time for man and earth. A number of texts will be presented that describe the events that are to come to earth. It is important to notice the references to darkness, earthquakes, fire, stars falling to earth, and volcanoes.

> *"A day of darkness and of gloominess, a day of clouds and of thick darkness, as the morning spread upon the mountains: a great people and a strong; there hath not been ever the like, neither shall be any more after it, even to the years of many generations. A fire devoureth before them; and behind them a flame burneth: the land is as the garden of Eden before them, and behind them a desolate wilderness; yea, and nothing shall escape them — The earth shall quake before them; the heavens shall tremble: the sun and the moon shall be dark, and the stars shall withdraw their shining — The sun shall be turned into darkness, and the moon into blood, before the great and the terrible day of the LORD come"* (Joel 2:2, 3, 10, 31)

"For the stars of heaven and the constellations thereof shall not give their light: the sun shall be darkened in his going forth, and the moon shall not cause her light to shine" (Isaiah 13:10)

"And I beheld when he had opened the sixth seal, and, lo, there was a great earthquake; and the sun became black as sackcloth of hair, and the moon became as blood; And the stars of heaven fell unto the earth, even as a fig tree casteth her untimely figs, when she is shaken of a mighty wind. And the heaven departed as a scroll when it is rolled together; and every mountain and island were moved out of their places" (Revelation 6:12-14)

"And the angel took the censer, and filled it with fire of the altar, and cast it into the earth: and there were voices, and thunderings, and lightnings, and an earthquake. And the seven angels which had the seven trumpets prepared themselves to sound. The first angel sounded, and there followed hail and fire mingled with blood, and they were cast upon the earth: and the third part of trees was burnt up, and all green grass was burnt up. And the second angel sounded, and as it were a great mountain burning with fire was cast into the sea: and the third part of the sea became blood; And the third part of the creatures which were in the sea, and had life, died; and the third part of the ships were destroyed. And the third angel sounded, and there fell a great star from heaven, burning as it were a lamp, and it fell upon the third part of the rivers, and upon the fountains of waters; And the name of the star is called Wormwood: and the third part of the waters became wormwood; and many men died of the waters, because they were made bitter. And the fourth angel sounded, and the third part

of the sun was smitten, and the third part of the moon, and the third part of the stars; so as the third part of them was darkened, and the day shone not for a third part of it, and the night likewise" (Revelation 8:5-12)

"And he opened the bottomless pit; and there arose a smoke out of the pit, as the smoke of a great furnace; and the sun and the air were darkened by reason of the smoke of the pit" (Revelation 9:2)

"And the same hour was there a great earthquake, and the tenth part of the city fell, and in the earthquake were slain of men seven thousand: and the remnant were affrighted, and gave glory to the God of heaven" (Revelation 11:13)

"And the fifth angel poured out his vial upon the seat of the beast; and his kingdom was full of darkness; and they gnawed their tongues for pain — And there were voices, and thunders, and lightnings; and there was a great earthquake, such as was not since men were upon the earth, so mighty an earthquake, and so great. And the great city was divided into three parts, and the cities of the nations fell: and great Babylon came in remembrance before God, to give unto her the cup of the wine of the fierceness of his wrath. And every island fled away, and the mountains were not found" (Revelation 16:10, 18-20)

The above prophecies taken from both the Old and New Testaments all present the same detail about the destruction and devastation of those days. It is very important to notice that Jesus Himself gave similar details.

"Immediately after the tribulation of those days shall the sun be darkened, and the moon shall not give her light, and the stars shall fall from heaven, and the powers of the heavens shall be shaken" (Matthew 24:29)

This period of devastation will end after the seven years when Jesus comes to claim His kingdom. Jesus is the only One who tells us what will happen to the earth and its inhabitants if He does not return to bring the Great Tribulation to a conclusion.

"For then shall be great tribulation, such as was not since the beginning of the world to this time, no, nor ever shall be. And except those days should be shortened, there should no flesh be saved: but for the elect's sake those days shall be shortened" (Matthew 24:21, 22)

You will notice that He said this will be the most terrible period of time since the beginning of the world. But most importantly, He says that every living creature on earth will die if those days are not brought to an end. In other words, the earth could once again become without form and void as darkness would cover a dead planet. But, praise God, Jesus is going to return and that great judgment will end before the earth returns to that condition!

It must have been another time of great tribulation on the earth that occurred between the first two verses of the Bible. There is no way of knowing how long the earth had suffered through numerous judgments before the final devastation that left it uninhabitable. The geological discoveries and fossil remains reveal that earth has gone through many catastrophes with a long period of time existing between some of them. The earth will have been suffering from Adam's sin for over 6,000 years before the final judgment comes against it. A period of millions or billions of years could very well have existed from the time that Lucifer fell back to the earth until it was in the condition presented in Genesis 1:2. God was certainly here all of that time!

The Bible does give some information about God bringing darkness and destruction upon the earth. He told Job about how the angels responded when they first viewed the earth after its creation: *"When the morning stars sang together, and all the sons of God shouted for joy"* (Job 38:7). He then immediately reminded Job of a judgment He had sent to the earth, *"When I made the cloud the garment thereof, and thick darkness a swaddlingband for it"* (Job 38:9). The same God who had given the beauty of the creation had also brought darkness through His judgments.

In Psalm 104 we are given a beautiful description of what took place prior to the six days and through the work of that great week. In verse two, God is seen as being covered by a garment of light as He stretched out the heavens. The angels were made as described in verse four. After the angels were created, verse five explains how God laid the foundations of the earth. From verses 7 – 18, the work of days one, two, and three is presented as He prepares water, grass, and trees for the creatures that will dwell on earth. The work of day four is given in verse 19 when He appoints the moon and sun to their work. God is then recognized for His great work in Psalm 104:30: *"Thou sendest forth thy spirit, they are created: and thou renewest the face of the earth"*. You will notice that God created new life and renewed the face of the earth. The Hebrew word that is translated 'renewest' is CHADASH. The same word was used in the following verses:

"And when Asa heard these words, and the prophecy of Oded the prophet, he took courage, and put away the abominable idols out of all the land of Judah and Benjamin, and out of the cities which he had taken from mount Ephraim, and renewed (CHADASH) the altar of the LORD, that was before the porch of the LORD" (2 Chronicles 15:8) (Emphasis mine)

"Create in me a clean heart, O God; and renew (CHADASH) a right spirit within me" (Psalm 51:10) (Emphasis mine)

The Apostle Peter presented some important information for those who believe that everything is continuing today as it has been since the beginning of the creation.

"Where is the promise of his coming? for since the fathers fell asleep, all things continue as they were from the beginning of the creation. For this they willingly are ignorant of, that by the word of God the heavens were of old, and the earth standing out of the water and in the water: Whereby the world that then was, being overflowed with water, perished: But the heavens and the earth, which are now, by the same word are kept in store, reserved unto fire against the day of judgment and perdition of ungodly men" (2 Peter 3:4-7)

Most of the YECs apply this text only to Noah's flood, but I am not so sure that it cannot refer back to the description given in Genesis 1:2. He speaks of the heavens being old and the earth standing out of the water and in the water. Then, he makes the statement that the world that existed then perished. But, did the world really perish because of Noah's flood? Life was preserved on the ark and the earth was repopulated with the same beings that existed prior to judgment.

All things have not continued in the same condition as they were created in Genesis 1:1. All things will not continue as they are today. The heavens and earth that we have today will be destroyed when God brings His final judgment against it.

> *"But the day of the Lord will come as a thief in the night; in the which the heavens shall pass away with a great noise, and the elements shall melt with fervent heat, the earth also and the works that are therein shall be burned up. Seeing then that all these things shall be dissolved, what manner of persons ought ye to be in all holy conversation and godliness, Looking for and hasting unto the coming of the day of God, wherein the heavens being on fire shall be dissolved, and the elements shall melt with fervent heat? Nevertheless we, according to his promise, look for new heavens and a new earth, wherein dwelleth righteousness"* (2 Peter 3:10-13)

There will be a new heaven and a new earth and they will never be touched by the affects of the sins of Lucifer or Adam! Lucifer will be forever in the lake of fire and all the descendants of Adam who accepted God's free gift of salvation will dwell on that new earth and be glorified forever.

❧

Our great eternal God is to be glorified by His acts of judgment as well as by His acts of creation! To the YECs, the only affect from Lucifer's sin is the temptation that he brought to Eve causing sin to enter the human race. According to them, the only consequence of Lucifer's rebellion against God was God casting him back to earth. Furthermore, any other judgment from God must wait until Satan is cast into the eternal lake of fire (Revelation 20:10). The RTRs see just the opposite in Scripture. They believe that God responded to Lucifer's sin just as He did to the sin of Adam by bringing judgment into each of their respective domains.

It should be emphasized that the earth becoming without form and void was not a result of the evil that was done BY Lucifer after he became Satan. It was what happened to the earth that Satan COULD NOT prevent from happening! He thought he could be equal to God, but he was an abject failure. It is no wonder that he will do everything he can to keep people from believing that a beautiful earth came to ruin because of him! Satan would like nothing more than for everyone to blame Adam for all the damage that has been done to earth through the cataclysms that have occurred because of sin. This falls right in line with the fact that Satan *"is a liar, and the father of it"* (John 8:44).

It is true that Adam's sin has brought death and much destruction to the earth on which we live. In spite of all the damage, however, the creation of God still brings great glory and honor to God as the Creator: *"The heavens declare the glory of God; and the firmament showeth his handywork"* (Psalm 19:1). It is not just the heavens, but the earth also that gives glory to Jesus Christ: *"For by him were all things created, that are in heaven, and that are in earth, visible and invisible, whether they be thrones, or dominions, or principalities, or powers: all things were created by him, and for him: And he is before all things, and by him all things consist"* (Colossians 1:16, 17).

The wrath of God against sin is great, but His love for each sinner is greater! His love for those who will accept His love will always overcome His wrath. There is coming a day when all the redeemed will gather around the throne of God and we will praise Jesus for His creation and then for His cross.

> *"The four and twenty elders fall down before him that sat on the throne, and worship him that liveth for ever and ever, and cast their crowns before the throne, saying, Thou art worthy, O Lord, to receive glory and honour and power: for thou hast created all things, and for thy pleasure they are and were created"* (Revelation 4:10, 11)

> *"And they sung a new song, saying, Thou art worthy to take the book, and to open the seals thereof: for thou wast slain, and hast redeemed us to God by thy blood out of every kindred, and tongue, and people, and nation"* (Revelation 5:9)

> *"Saying with a loud voice, Worthy is the Lamb that was slain to receive power, and riches, and wisdom, and strength, and honour, and glory, and blessing"* (Revelation 5:12)

It is His redemption that will remove all the damage done to His creation by the sins of Lucifer and the sins of Adam's race. He will be praised for His acts of creation and for His acts of redemption on that day. He is just as worthy now!

Each reader is encouraged to do now what will then be done by everyone!

> *"And every creature which is in heaven, and on the earth, and under the earth, and such as are in the sea, and all that are in them, heard I saying, Blessing, and honour, and glory, and power, be unto him that sitteth upon the throne, and unto the Lamb for ever and ever. And the four beasts said, Amen. And the four and twenty elders fell down and worshipped him that liveth for ever and ever"* (Revelation 5:13, 14)

It has been my intention in this chapter to reveal the faithfulness of God in dealing with any sin that is committed against Him: *"The LORD is slow to anger, and great in power, and will not at all acquit the wicked: the LORD hath his way in the whirlwind and in the storm, and the clouds are the dust of his feet"* (Nahum 1:3). God's judgment against Lucifer's rebellion resulted in the earth becoming without form and void. God renovated the earth into a beautiful place in the six days work and created Adam to have dominion over it. When Adam and Eve sinned, God was forced to once again send judgment to the earth and all who dwelt on it. The YECs do not accept all these beliefs and their criticisms will be confronted in the next chapter.

Chapter 6
ANSWERING THE CRITICS

In an ideal and perfect world everyone would believe the truth and there would be no need for disagreements. We do not live in such a world, however, and there are great differences in what some believe to be the truth. There are many doctrines that many believe are so clearly presented in the Bible that everyone should agree with their interpretations. Yet, there are great differences in what is being taught on some of these very cardinal beliefs.

Some disagree because they pick and choose which verses they will use and which they will ignore. Others will not agree because they do not consider the Bible to be the inspired, infallible, and inerrant Word of God and thus it is not the final authority for their beliefs. So, they use logic and human understanding to determine what they believe. There are others who may all use the same verses yet interpret them differently in reaching divergent views.

Some of the differences that exist between the teachings of the YECs and RTRs about the age of the earth have been presented in the previous chapters. However, there are many other things that they totally agree on. Both groups believe in the work of the six days resulting in a beautiful earth that was ready for habitation. They also agree that God created every species that presently lives on earth just a few thousand years ago. Both groups are equally adamant against any teaching of the solar system and universe coming about by any means other than the creative acts of God. The same is true for their opposition to any teaching concerning the evolution of the species. There are no disagreements on the fact that God brought a global flood in the days of Noah. Most importantly, the vast majority of the ones who hold each of these views believe that salvation is only available in Jesus Christ when one accepts Him through faith and repentance.

It is the perceived age of the earth that is the main area of disagreement between the two groups. The YECs believe that everything that has been created came into being just a few thousand years ago. This includes the earth and its inhabitants, as well as the moon, the solar system and the entire universe. The RTRs see a reason to accept an old age for the earth and the rest of the physical creation, but a relatively young creation of species (including Adam's race) dwelling on the earth. Most YECs are very adamant in their disagreements with the RTRs. Since I consider myself an RTR, YECs teach against what I believe.

It is very important to me that I teach the truth about any subject. The wise man wrote, *"Buy the truth, and sell it not"* (Proverbs 23:23). That verse simply teaches that we should settle for no less than the truth no matter how much it costs us. Also, when we know that we have the truth, we should not sell it no matter how much we are offered for it. If someone disagrees with what I believe, it is incumbent on me to search out their reasons to determine if they are right. If I am wrong, I need to know that! I will then be accurate in what I teach in the future, and I can make corrections to anyone that I might have misled in the past.

I am aware of three main ministries dedicated to the teaching of the YECs. It is these three ministries on which I have conducted my research. The first is the Institute of Creation Research (ICR) located in El Cajon, California. Dr. John Morris is the Director. He is the son of Henry Morris who co-authored *The Genesis Flood* in 1961. *The Genesis Flood* gave birth to the modern day 'young earth' movement. Ken Ham organized the second, Answers In Genesis (AIG), in the 1980s and has the Creation Museum in Petersburg, Kentucky (near Cincinnati, Ohio.) Kent Hovind organized the third, Creation Science Evangelism (CSE), in 1989 in Pensacola, Florida, where he also built Dinosaur Adventure Land theme park. All of these ministries have provided much information refuting what they call the "Gap Theory". Since they refer to the belief of the RTRs as the Gap Theory, I will do the same in this chapter.

I have watched videos, read many articles in various books and periodicals, and heard Bible teachers repeat what these organizations have presented as flaws in the Gap Theory. After carefully studying their objections, I have yet to find even one of the supposed errors as having any justification or merit.

I attended a presentation by Kent Hovind from CSE where he made the statement that the Gap Theory is 'one of the most dangerous heresies being taught today.' I made a phone call to

Mr. Hovind's office at CSE in Pensacola hoping to find some verifiable basis for his accusation. I asked for any documents Mr. Hovind would recommend that would explain his reason for entirely dismissing the Gap Theory. The clerk immediately referred me to Hovind's own booklet, *The Gap Theory*, co-written with Stephen Lawwell. I was assured that this booklet would show the justification for Hovind's belief that the Gap Theory was so dangerous. I ordered and read the booklet, but it gave little more information than had been gleaned from other sources.

The YECs are very critical of what the RTRs believe. For their criticism to be valid, some of their points of opposition should have some merit. Keeping an open mind, I have not yet found one item of contention that has any validity! In this chapter I will be presenting the charges made by these organizations against the Gap Theory and will then present my answers to the critics.

Attitudes Against Those Who Believe In The Gap Theory

The attitude that Kent Hovind has towards those who believe there is a gap of time between the first two verses of the Bible is revealed in the Preface that he wrote in his book *The Gap Theory*.

> This godless theory resulted in the rise of such philosophies as communism, humanism, and Nazism. The acceptance of the gap theory opened the floodgates for these ideologies, which have caused untold suffering as well as hundreds of millions of deaths in the last two centuries.[37]

What evidence does he give to justify these charges? None! He simply states that this theory as to how God created the universe has caused millions of people to be killed. That is quite a charge!

I was attending a Bible study being taught by a dear friend of mine who believes in the young earth. He provided a handout to his class that included the statement, "The Gap Theory is scientifically impossible and theologically dangerous." When I later asked him about the source of this statement, he told me that it came from the college that he attended. How can human beings determine what things are 'scientifically impossible' for God to perform? Was a global flood scientifically possible? Was it scientifically possible for the Red Sea to open up with a wall of water standing on each side while the children of Israel walked across on dry ground? How many thousands of other works does the Bible describe as having been performed by God that would be deemed impossible by unbelievers?

We know that God placed a curse on everything on earth after the sin of Adam and Eve resulting in death and destruction. The earth they were placed on is doomed to final destruction because of their sin. Why is it theologically dangerous to believe that there was an original creation that was destroyed by the judgment of God following Lucifer's sin? The Bible says that God never changes: *"For I am the LORD, I change not"* (Malachi 3:6). What was the result from Lucifer's sin? Is it theologically safe to believe that God had no reaction other than casting Lucifer back to earth? Why would God be so harsh in judgment against Adam's sin while bringing no judgment because of the sin of Lucifer?

All who believe in the creative works of God believe that He is an eternal One who has always existed. There has never been a time when God did not exist. Yet, the YECs believe that God never performed a creative act until just a few thousand years ago. Thus, they believe that we humans are part of His first creative acts. The Gap Theory teaches that God could possibly have been busy as Creator for millions or billions of years. Therefore, we are the last of His creative works, not among the first. God is glorified by the geological discoveries of events dated millions of years ago just as He is by today's sunrise or sunset! Which view is really theologically dangerous and fails to recognize all His wonderful works?

The holy Bible is, of course, the basis for all truth. Even so, dedicated Bible students use various study aids in addition to the Bible in determining their beliefs. This can include word studies from the original Hebrew, Greek, or Aramaic languages. What has been learned through personal study will then be used to teach others. In his video *"The Age Of The Earth"*, Hovind stated that when teachers refer to the original language it 'probably means they are members of a cult.' He also made the following statement in his book *The Gap Theory*.

> If the gap theory were true, the average person must not be capable of reading the Bible and understanding it without some guru or priest telling them what it really means. This is an earmark of nearly all cults.[38]

He also makes references to the original language in his video and book referenced above, but he fails to explain why it is acceptable for him and not for others!

These are just some of the examples of the ridiculous charges that are made against those who believe there could be a gap of time between the first two verses of the Bible. Some YECs accuse proponents of the Gap Theory of causing the deaths of millions, of being dangerous in theological matters, and even of being members of a cult. It is an example of the principle that if you cannot legitimately refute the message then you attack the messenger. By creating a loss of confidence in an individual, you will normally create a loss of confidence in what he is teaching.

The Age of The Gap Theory

The YECs teach that the Gap Theory was developed after geologists came up with their geological periods showing that the earth was very old in the 16th and 17th centuries. According to them, some who had previously believed the earth was very young accepted the teaching of the geologists and had to come up with an explanation that would allow the Bible to still be accepted as true. Thus, they teach that the Gap Theory was developed in an effort to accept the findings of the geologists while also holding to the biblical account. If this is true, then the Gap Theory was really determined by science rather than Scripture. The truth is that many believed in the Gap Theory for hundreds (or thousands) of years before the geological tables were developed.

Kent Hovind teaches that Thomas Chalmers (1780-1847), a notable Scottish theologian and first moderator of the Free Church of Scotland, was the first proponent of the Gap Theory.[39] Ken Ham's organization teaches that the theory can be traced back to the rather obscure writings of the Dutchman

Episcopius (1583-1643).[40]   These men were teachers of the theory, but the theory predates them.

One of the most brilliant writers of the past century was Dr. Erich Sauer, Director of the Bible School, Wiedenest, Germany. Though he wrote in German, Mr. G. H. Lang was allowed to translate his five books into the English language. Sauer's most notable books were *The Dawn Of World Redemption* concerning the Old Testament, and its companion about the New Testament, *The Triumph Of The Crucified*. Dr. Sauer referred to the Gap Theory and gave some historical information about it.

> In both old and more recent times there have been God-enlightened men who in this connexion have expressed the conjecture that the work of the six days of Genesis 1 was properly a work of restoration, but not the original creation of the earth, and that originally man had the task, as a servant of the Lord and as ruler of the creation, in moral opposition to Satan, to recover for God the outwardly renewed earth, through the spreading abroad of his race and his lordship over the earth.

> In this way it might be possible to find a reconciliation between the Biblical account of the world's origin and that of modern natural philosophy. Traces of such an explanation of the record of creation are found in ancient Christian literature as early as the time of the church father Augustine (about A. D. 400). In the seventh century it was maintained by the Anglo-Saxon poet Caedmon. About A. D. 1000, King Edgar of England espoused it. In the seventeenth century it was

specially emphasized by the mystic Jacob Boehme. In the year 1814 it was developed by the Scottish scholar Dr. Chalmers, and in 1833 further by the English professor of mineralogy William Buckland.

There are also very many German upholders of this teaching, as for instance, the professor of geology Freiherr von Huene (Tubingen); and well-known are the English scholar G. H. Pember, and also the Scofield "Reference Bible", so widely circulated in all English-speaking lands. From the Catholic side there are Cardinal Wiseman and the philosopher Friedrich von Schlegel.[41]

So, Sauer introduces those who have believed in the Gap Theory all the way back to the fourth century. Many others have presented similar information.

A few of the early Church Fathers accepted this interpretation and based some of their doctrines upon it. It is true that both they and their Jewish antecedents used arguments which to us seem at times to have no force whatever, but this is not the issue. The truth is, as we shall see, that the idea of a once ordered world having been brought to ruin as a consequence of divine judgment just prior to the creation of Adam, was apparently quite widespread. It was not debated: it was merely held by some and not by others.[42]

Beginning in the mid to late 6th century b.c., the Jewish people began compiling commentaries and explanations of their best teachers regarding the Old Testament. This compilation continued for about 1500 years in a document called the Midrash. In his great work, *The Legends Of The Jews*, Louis Ginsberg referenced the Midrash in his volume that covered the period of time from the Creation to Jacob. He gave this excerpt on Genesis 1.

> Nor is this world inhabited by man the first of things earthly created by God. He made several other worlds before ours, but He destroyed them all, because He was pleased with none until He created ours.[43]

There are other documents and records from the early days of the Christian era which reveal that others held to the belief that the original earth had been destroyed by the judgment of God.

> Another piece of substantiating evidence is to be found in the Targum of Onkelos, the earliest of the Aramaic Versions of the Old Testament written by Hebrew Scholars. According to the Babylonian Talmud, Onkelos was a proselyte, the son of a man named Galonicas, and although he was the composer of the Targum which bears his name, he is held actually to have received it from Rabbi Eliezer and Rabbi Yehoshua, both of whom lived towards the end of the first and the beginning of the second century A. D. However, since in the Jerusalem Talmud the very same things is related by the same authorities (and almost in the same words) of the proselyte Aquila of Pontes, whose Greek version of the Bible was used by the Greek speaking Jews down to the time of Justinian, it is sometimes argued that Onkelos is but another name for Aquila. Aquila Ponticus was a relative of the Emperor Hadrian, living in the second century B. C. Thus even if Onkelos is not yet completely identified, the Targum attributed to him must still be placed early in the second cen-

tury B. C. His translation into Aramaic of Genesis 1:2 was "and the earth was laid waste" an interpretation of the original Hebrew which leaves little room for doubt that Onkelos understood this to mean that something had occurred between verse 1 and verse 2 to reduce the earth to this desolated condition.[44]

In the excerpt from his book *The Dawn Of World Redemption*, Sauer mentioned Caedmon who was an English poet who died about 680 A. D. Caedmon wrote about Genesis and the creation and presented the view that man had really been introduced in order to replace the angels which had conducted themselves so badly. He presented the view that the earth had been ruined and the fallen angels were responsible for the catastrophe.[45]

It is obvious with all the references given above that the belief in the Gap Theory was held a long time before geologists discovered the layers of fossil remains indicating an old earth. It was first believed by people who only had the Bible to study! Those who held the view simply had their beliefs confirmed when geologists began to make their discoveries. D. F. Payne of the University of Sheffield, England, acknowledged that the belief in the Gap Theory grew after the discoveries of the geologists began to be published.

> The gap theory itself, as a matter of exegesis, antedated the scientific challenge, but the latter gave it a new impetus.[46]

Numerous other Bible and Hebrew scholars from the 18th century wrote about their views that there was a gap between the first two verses of the Bible.[47]

1. William Buckland wrote *"Geology and Minerology Considered With Reference to Natural Theology"* in 1836.

2. J. H. Kurtz wrote *"The Bible and Astronomy"* in 1853.

3. Franz Delitzsch wrote *"New Commentary on Genesis"* in 1888. At that time he did not believe in a gap of time between Genesis 1:1 and 1:2. Later he wrote *"A System of Biblical Psychology"* in 1899 where he stated his belief in the concept of a rebellion in heaven and a judgment brought upon the earth as a consequence prior to the creation of Adam. Thus, while he still did not propose that 'was' should be translated 'became', he did admit that this is really what had happened. Delitzsch was considered one of the greatest Hebrew scholars of his day.

4. Fr. H. Reusch wrote *"Nature and The Bible"* in 1886.

To this number you can add George Gleig, E. B. Pusey, J. Oliver Buswell, A. Dillman, S. R. Driver, John Skinner, and many, many more.

There were two notable publications in the early part of the 19th century that led to the spread of the Gap Theory. In 1909, Dr. C. I. Scofield published his Scofield Reference Bible where the footnotes presented the theory of the original earth having been destroyed and the six days work being a reconstruction of the earth with a new creation of living beings. Dr. Clarence Larkin wrote his classic *Dispensational Truth* in 1918 where he presented in detail the ruin that came upon the earth and the restoration that followed in the six days work.

The Gap Theory has been under serious attack in recent years by those who believe in a young earth. In spite of their opposition, however, a great number of theologians still hold to this belief as attested to by Kent Hovind.

Regardless of the reason, the gap theory has gained considerable support from several modern theologians. These theologians, such as Arthur C. Custance, author of *Without Form and Void* (1970), and well known preachers Billy Graham, Peter Ruckman, and John Hagee, have adopted the gap theory, in one form or another.[48]

In his presentations, Hovind has also included Dr. James Dobson as also agreeing with the Gap Theory.

The accusation by the YECs that those who hold to the Gap Theory only do so because of the geological ages is not true. The geological discoveries only validate that the biblical interpretations of the RTRs is consistent with what has been found on the earth. Nor is it true that the Gap Theory is a belief that came about in the last 200 years. All evidence points to the Gap Theory being a belief that has been held for thousands of years. We do not know what Adam believed about the age of the earth on which he lived, nor do we know what Moses believed about the age of the earth whose creation he wrote about in Genesis!

YECs Refute The Scriptural Proof of the Gap Theory Proponents

In Chapter 2, numerous scriptures were referenced that present the truth that the earth was NOT created without form and void, but became that way due to the judgment of God following the rebellion of Lucifer. The YECs are aware of some of these verses and have tried to offer interpretations that would support their belief in a young earth, created only a few thousand years ago. In fairness to them, I will present their refutations.

It is absolutely imperative for the YECs to believe that the first two verses of the Bible were part of the first day in Genesis 1. If they ever concede that those two verses describe the original condition and that verse three begins the work of day one, their entire theory will be destroyed. Yet, it is not until verse three that the words *"And God said"* are used for the first time. These same words are used to begin all of the other days in Genesis 1. All legitimate rules of biblical interpretation require that the work on day one begins in Genesis 1:3 and not 1:1.

YECs are also adamant that the word 'was' in Genesis 1:2 must describe the earth as it had been since it was created. All it really does, however, is present the condition of the earth as it existed at that point in time. There is no reference in this verse as to how it had become that way. As shown previously, the condition of being 'without form and void' as described in verse two is not consistent with the word 'created' as used in verse one, which means 'to form and fashion'. In 1888, Franz Delitzsch quoted another Hebrew scholar, August Dillman, as presenting the following view.[49]

> A created chaos is a nonentity. If once the notion of an Almighty God is so far developed that He is also conceived of as the author of matter, the application of chaos in the doctrine of creation must consequently cease. For such a God will not first create the matter and then the form, but both together.

If it were true that God created the earth without form and void, it would be the only thing He ever did that was not perfectly done!

Many who hold to the Gap Theory use the command God gave Adam to *"Be fruitful, and multiply, and replenish the earth"* (Genesis 1:28) as possible proof that the earth was previously populated, and that Adam was to replenish, or repopulate, it. Kent Hovind attempted to prove that this is an invalid interpretation.

> Genesis 1:28 is undoubtedly the verse most quoted by gap theorists. Genesis 1:28 *"And God blessed them, and God said unto them, Be fruitful, and multiply, and replenish the earth, and subdue it: and have dominion over the fish of the sea, and over the fowl of the air, and over every living thing that moveth upon the earth."* Much of the validity drawn from this verse centers on the usage of the word replenish. Gap theorists believe that this is God's command for Adam and Eve to refill, or repopulate, the earth, assuming the previous inhabitants of the earth were destroyed in the Genesis 1:2 catastrophe.

> The problem that gap theorists encounter stems from misunderstanding the word *replenish*. The Hebrew word used here is MALE, which means "to fill." In 1611, the time of the King James translation, English dictionaries defined the word *replenish* as "to supply fully, to fill." Nearly a century later, a second definition arose, "to fill or build up again." Most dictionaries still list both meanings. If the author of Genesis 1 had been attempting to convey the idea that God wanted Adam and Eve to repopulate the earth, he would have used the Hebrew word SHANA, which means "to fill again."[50]

This is an interesting argument. What the word 'replenish' meant in the dictionaries in 1611, however, is not the issue.

The word that was used in the original biblical text is all that matters.

Hovind states that if God had wanted to tell Adam to "fill it again" He would have used the word SHANA instead of MALE. Well, we know for certain that God told Noah in Genesis 9:1 to repopulate the earth. What word do you suppose was used then? It was exactly the same that was spoken to Adam, *"Be fruitful, and multiply, and replenish* (MALE) *the earth"* (Genesis 9:1) (Emphasis mine). The word MALE was used for Noah to refill the earth giving us just reason to believe that God also meant for Adam to refill the earth when those words were first spoken to him.

God remembered the earth when it was populated with dinosaurs and many other prehistoric creatures before they all died because of Lucifer's sin. He wanted His renewed earth to be populated again, so the command was given to Adam. In Noah's day, it was the sins of man that brought death to all who were outside of the ark. Thus, the command to replenish the earth was given to Noah. It is no coincidence that the exact words were used for Adam in Genesis 1:28 and for Noah in Genesis 9:1!

The belief that the earth was created perfectly and then became without form and void at a later time is further justified in Isaiah 45:18: *"For thus saith the LORD that created the heavens; God himself that formed the earth and made it; he hath established it, he created it not in vain, he formed it to be inhabited: I am the LORD; and there is none else."* Of particular interest is the phrase *"he created it not in vain, he formed it to be inhabited."* The word 'vain' was translated in this verse from

TOHU which was translated 'without form' in Genesis 1:2. If that same translation was used in Isaiah, one would have "He created it not without form, He formed it to be inhabited." Regardless, it proves the earth was not created without form, so it must have become that way at a later time. But, Hovind has an explanation for this also.

> In recent years, Isaiah 45:18 has become the verse to which most gap theorists appeal in defense of their view. The debate concerning this verse surrounds Isaiah's use of the phrase, "he created it not in vain." The words "in vain," translated from the Hebrew TOHU, also occur in Genesis 1:2 where it is translated "without form." Gap theorists conclude that God did not create the earth without form (TOHU), as described in Genesis 1:2, but that it became without form (TOHU). - - No where does Scripture use the word TOHU to describe a result of God's judgment.[51]

He does a good job of presenting what the Gap Theory proponents believe, but once again his conclusions are flawed.

Hovind wrote that "No where does Scripture use the word TOHU to describe a result of God's judgment". This statement is easily refuted in Scripture. In Isaiah 34:8 *"the day of the Lord's vengeance"* produced the condition of TOHU where it is translated *"line of confusion"* (Isaiah 34:11). In Jeremiah 4:23, the prophet saw the earth TOHU (translated "without form") as a result of being *"broken down at the presence of the Lord, and by his fierce anger"* (Jeremiah 4:26). The word TOHU is found a total of 22 times and there are numerous other instances where it is used to describe the result of God's judgment. Mr. Hovind's assertion is completely false.

Ken Ham also erroneously attempted to explain away Isaiah 45:18 in an article from AIG. He stated that God was talking about Israel and not the earth.

> Isaiah 45:18 (often quoted by gappists) is rendered in the KJV "he created it not in vain (TOHU), he formed it to be inhabited." In the context, Isaiah is speaking about Israel, God's people, and His grace in restoring them. He did not choose His people in order to destroy them, but to be their God and for them to be His people.[52]

Ham totally misses the point that God was assuring the people that the One who took an earth that had become without form and void and made it a beautiful earth again would also be able to gather His people Israel back into a prosperous nation after their judgment had ended.

The relationship of Jeremiah 4:23-27 and Isaiah 34:11 to Genesis 1:2 was also presented in Chapter 2. These are the only three places in Scripture where the words TOHU and BOHU are found together. In the verses found in Jeremiah and Isaiah the condition is presented as having come about because of the judgment of God. Using the rules of Bible interpretation, consistency would lead one to believe that the words would mean the same thing in Genesis 1:2 as well. An article from AIG admits that judgment caused the condition described by Jeremiah and Isaiah but denies that the same usage can be applied in Genesis.

> Though the expression "TOHU and BOHU" in Isaiah 34:11 and Jeremiah 4:23 speaks of a formlessness and emptiness resulting from divine judgment for sin, this

meaning is not implicit in the expression itself but is gained from the particular contexts in which it occurs. It is not valid therefore to infer that same meaning from Genesis 1:2, where the context does not suggest any judgment.[53]

The Bible is not of any private interpretation: *"Knowing this first, that no prophecy of the scripture is of any private interpretation"* (2 Peter 1:20). How words are used in one part of the Bible can instruct the student on how they are to be interpreted in other locations. The words TOHU and BOHU appear together in two locations as describing the results from the judgment of an angry God. They are never used to describe the result of His creative powers! Therefore, to be consistent, the other use of these words in Genesis 1:2 describes the judgment of God and not His creative acts.

Kent Hovind of CSE had another explanation for the account found in Jeremiah concerning the earth being without form and void.

Gap theorists frequently quote Jeremiah 4:23, 24 in their attempt to depict the desolate earth of Genesis 1:2. They believe that the prophet Jeremiah is describing in detail God's act of judgment upon the "first" earth. — The phrase "without form, and void" seems to imply an association with Genesis 1:2, but the word earth in this verse is not a reference to the planet earth. Earth in this verse refers to the land of Judah. – These two verses, when read in the context of the whole chapter, reveal the prophet Jeremiah's insight into the coming destruction of Judah by the Babylonian armies.[54]

There are numerous flaws in his presentation. Jeremiah said he beheld the ERETS and not Judah. It is the same word translated 'earth' in Genesis 1:1. While the Babylonians did bring great judgment upon Judah, the land never became without form and void. There was never a time as a result of the Babylonian invasion when *"there was no man, and all the birds of the heaven were fled"* as described in Jeremiah 4:25. This is another example of using unverified and invalid teachings in an effort to counter the belief of the Gap Theory.

Several efforts of noted YECs in explaining away the verses used by those who believe there is a gap between the first verses of the Bible have been presented. It has been shown that none of their points of criticism have <u>any</u> validity. It should be obvious that if the RTRs are wrong in their interpretation and understanding of Scripture someone should be able to present some evidence that would reveal an error. All the accusations against the Gap Theory have no substance!

<u>YECs Present Their Own Scriptures Against The Gap Theory</u>

The ones who hold to the belief of a young earth have not only tried to refute the verses used by those who teach the Gap Theory, but they also use other verses in an effort to prove the earth is very young. The same arguments and explanations using verses that supposedly rebut the Gap Theory have been presented in numerous books and articles that I have read. I have heard several Bible teachers repeat these same verses to promote their belief of a young earth. Their arguments will be presented with my discussion of their interpretations.

The main argument of the YECs against the Gap Theory is that the RTRs place death before the sin of Adam. If the fossils, dinosaurs, etc., all lived on an earth that was prior to the six days work, then obviously they had died before the earth became without form and void. To the YECs this is impossible since they believe there had never been death until Adam sinned. There are two main verses that they base their belief on.

> *"Wherefore, as by one man sin entered into the world, and death by sin; and so death passed upon all men, for that all have sinned"* (Romans 5:12)

> *"For since by man came death, by man came also the resurrection of the dead. For as in Adam all die, even so in Christ shall all be made alive"* (1 Corinthians 15:21, 22)

I have heard several people make the statement that "Romans 5:12 is fatal to the Gap Theory." Since they believe that death was introduced because of Adam's sin, then dinosaurs or any other creatures could not have died before Adam sinned. Ken Ham of AIG, Kent Hovind of CSE, and John Morris of ICR all hold this view.

> The Gap Theory puts death, disease, and suffering before the Fall, contrary to Scripture, *"Wherefore, as by one man [Adam] sin entered into the world, and death by sin; and so death passed upon all men, for that all have sinned"* (Romans 5:12). From this we understand that there could not have been human sin or death before Adam.[55]

The Gap Theory puts death before Adam's sin violating Romans 5:12 and 1 Corinthians 15:21. Therein lies the Gap Theory's greatest error, the placement of sin and death prior to the existence of Adam.[56]

"For since by man came death, by man came also the resurrection of the dead. For as in Adam all die, even so in Christ shall all be made alive" (1 Corinthians 15:21, 22). The Bible plainly teaches that *"the wages of sin is death"* (Romans 6:23). Before Adam and Eve rebelled, animals ate only plants (Genesis 1:30). Death came as a result of sin and the curse: *"For in the day that thou eatest thereof* (the forbidden tree) *thou shalt surely die"* (Genesis 2:17). The first death in all of creation occurred when God provided Adam and Eve animal skins for clothing. Sin always brings death (Romans 5:12)[57]

First of all, these verses have nothing to do with the death of animals even though Adam's sin did bring death upon animals. Romans 5:12 is presenting the truth that all men need to be saved because *"death passed upon all men"* due to Adam's sin. The verse in 1 Corinthians presents the truth that each one who has received the salvation presented in Romans 5 will one day be resurrected by the power of Jesus Christ. If that verse is teaching that animals died because of Adam's sin, then it is also teaching that every dinosaur, dog, cat, etc., will be resurrected. To use these verses about salvation and the second coming of Jesus to determine the time of the death of animals is a gross misrepresentation of Scripture! They each admit that sin always results in death but totally ignore the fact that Lucifer committed the first sin and never consider any death that came from his sin.

It is true that Adam's sin did bring death to him and all the species that were created on days 5 and 6. The earth was a beautiful place at the conclusion of the six days work. All of that earth was cursed as a result of Adam's sin (Genesis 3:14-19). The verses from Romans 5:12 and 1 Corinthians 5:21 refer to the death that came on Adam's race and have no reference to anything that might have happened prior to that time. The questions remain, however, whether there had ever been death before the creation of Adam or was death possible on that newly renovated earth even without Adam's sin?

When God placed Adam in the Garden of Eden, He provided four types of trees: *"And out of the ground made the LORD God to grow every tree that is pleasant to the sight, and good for food; the tree of life also in the midst of the garden, and the tree of knowledge of good and evil"* (Genesis 2:9). There were evidently many trees that were (1) pleasant to the sight or (2) good for food. There was one (3) tree of life in the very middle of the garden and one (4) tree of the knowledge of good and evil. The first three types of trees were given to Adam for him to freely eat from, but God commanded that he abstain from the tree of the knowledge of good and evil.

> *"And the LORD God took the man, and put him into the garden of Eden to dress it and to keep it. And the LORD God commanded the man, saying, Of every tree of the garden thou mayest freely eat: But of the tree of the knowledge of good and evil, thou shalt not eat of it: for in the day that thou eatest thereof thou shalt surely die"* (Genesis 2:15-17)

It should be obvious that God intended for Adam to be able to eat from the tree of life, but why was it needed?

After Adam and Eve had sinned and God found them hiding in the midst of the garden, He pronounced a curse upon the serpent, Adam and Eve, all the animals, and even the ground (Genesis 3:14-19). The last curse He announced was when He removed the possibility of them eating from the tree of life.

> *"And the LORD God said, Behold, the man is become as one of us, to know good and evil: and now, lest he put forth his hand, and take also of the tree of life, and eat, and live for ever: Therefore the LORD God sent him forth from the garden of Eden, to till the ground from whence he was taken. So he drove out the man; and he placed at the east of the garden of Eden Cherubims, and a flaming sword which turned every way, to keep the way of the tree of life"* (Genesis 3:22-24)

It is evident from these verses that the purpose of the tree of life was to allow those who ate from it to live forever. If there was no death, then why would Adam even need it? Once he had sinned the tree was taken away to keep him from eating from it and living forever in a sinful state. Thus, death was possible before Adam and Eve sinned but it could not be escaped after their transgression. The key word is "surely" when God said, *"for in the day that thou eatest thereof thou shalt surely die"* (Genesis 2:17).

We do not know how much Adam really understood about the meaning of the word 'die'. We understand that death means separation and there are three possible deaths that can happen to a human. The first is physical death where the soul and spirit is separated from the body (Ecclesiastes 12:7). The second is eternal death where the body, soul, and spirit of the lost are eternally separated from God in the lake of fire (Revelation 20:14; 21:8). The third is spiritual death that occurs when a person becomes lost in sin at the point of accountability and will be separated from God spiritually until salvation is received through Jesus Christ (Ephesians 2:1).

God had promised that Adam would die the day that he ate of the forbidden tree. He did not die physically that day because he lived over 900 years. He was not cast into the lake of fire, so he did not die the second death on the day that he ate of that tree. He was, however, spiritually separated from God resulting in his trying to hide from the presence of God. While Adam died spiritually on the very day of his sin, the sin also assured that he would one day die physically, and without faith in the redemption found in God, he would spend eternity in hell.

It was spiritual death which Romans 5:12 is referring to since Adam's sin brought that death upon all men. That is why all men need to be saved. However, it is physical death that 1 Corinthians 15:21-22 refers to since Jesus will gloriously resurrect the dead bodies of all who accept His salvation. To attempt to use these verses to determine the time of the death of dinosaurs is a gross misuse of Scripture!

Another verse prominently used by the YECs in their effort to prove that the six days work was the very beginning of God's creative acts is found at the conclusion of Genesis 1.

"And God saw every thing that he had made, and, behold, it was very good. And the evening and the morning were the sixth day" (Genesis 1:31)

It is the use of the words 'very good' that causes them dismay. They believe that God would not see it as very good if Lucifer had already fallen, or if the earth contained the fossil remains of pre-existing life on the earth.

Ken Ham presents the argument that God would not call His creation very good if it was built on the dead remains of a previous creation.

> Some theorists also put the fall of Satan in this supposed period (between the first 2 verses of the Bible.) But any rebellion of Satan during this gap of time contradicts God's description of His completed creation on Day 6 as all being "very good." Genesis 1:29, 30 teaches us that animals and man were originally created to eat plants, which is consistent with God's description of His creation as "very good." But how could a fossil record, which gives evidence of disease, violence, death, and decay (fossils have been found of animals apparently fighting and certainly eating each other), be described as "very good"?[58]

Kent Hovind wrote that Lucifer could not have sinned prior to the end of the six days if God saw everything as "very good." He has a very imaginative interpretation of Job 38:7 where it is stated that the angels shouted for joy when they saw God lay the foundations of the earth.

> Job 38:7 explains that "all the sons of God," celebrated a portion of God's creation. The "sons of God shouted for joy" because God had just "laid the foundations of the earth." This clearly shows that Satan was created prior to the earth's foundation being laid. The

"foundations" probably refer to "land," appearing on the third day of creation (Genesis 1:9). The creation of Satan most likely occurred on the first, second, or possibly third day of God's creation. God said in Genesis 1:31 that He *"saw every thing that he had made, and, behold, it was very good."* If Satan had already fallen, God could not have made this statement.[59]

It is difficult to understand how he could believe that laying the foundations of the earth was talking about the third day and not the creation described in Genesis 1:1. It is even more amazing that he believes that Lucifer was created on one of the first three days of the six days work, yet that event was not included in the text. He based his interpretations on the belief that the six days work was the beginning of God's work in creation. When one starts with an invalid belief and tries to find evidence for that belief, the proof will be just as invalid!

The main mistake that both Ham and Hovind make is that they believe they are qualified to know what is "very good" in the sight of God. No man can determine that (Isaiah 40:13, 14; 1 Corinthians 2:16). God stated in Isaiah that His thoughts are far above ours: *"For as the heavens are higher than the earth, so are my ways higher than your ways, and my thoughts than your thoughts"* (Isaiah 55:9).

God saw the earth without form and void in Genesis 1:2. After He had finished His six days work, He saw a beautiful earth perfectly prepared for the new creation He had placed on it. It is no wonder He saw it as very good! The presence of fossils and bones from previous life that had once lived on the earth would not distract from what He had done in those six days. Neither would the presence of Satan if Adam would only obey the commands of God.

The YECs also teach that the Gap Theory can't be true because of God's institution of the Sabbath day. They use the following verses to bolster their claim.

> *"For in six days the LORD made heaven and earth, the sea, and all that in them is, and rested the seventh day: wherefore the LORD blessed the sabbath day, and hallowed it."* (Exodus 20:11)

> *"It* (Sabbath) *is a sign between me and the children of Israel for ever: for in six days the LORD made heaven and earth, and on the seventh day he rested, and was refreshed"* (Exodus 31:17) (Emphasis mine)

Ham and Hovind both use these verses in an effort to prove that everything that has ever been created occurred on those six days.

> Believing in the gap theory presents a number of problems and inconsistencies, especially for a Christian. It is inconsistent with God creating everything in six days, as Scripture says in Exodus 20:11. Thus the creation of the heavens and the earth (Genesis 1:1) and the sea and all that is in them (the rest of the creation) was completed in six days.[60]

> In Exodus 20:11 and Exodus 31:17, God says He created all things in six days. The phrase "and all that in them is" included Satan, the angels, stars, space, earth, plants, animals, and man.[61]

They totally ignore the fact that the word create is not even found in those verses! As presented in Chapter 2, the word for 'create' is BARA and means to form and fashion out of nothing. The word for 'made' is ASAH and refers to taking pre-existing material and giving it a new purpose. After Genesis 1:1, the word BARA is not used until the fifth and sixth days. On the other days, the work of God was described with ASAH. The work of the six days involved re-making the surface of the earth for the new life He created to live on it.

The Sabbath is based on the work that God did in the six days. On day two, He made the firmament and called it "Heaven" (Genesis 1:8). On the third day, He separated the waters and called the dry land "Earth" and the water "Seas" (Genesis 1:10). The phrase "and all that in them is" is simply referring to the life that God created on the fifth and sixth days. The institution of the Sabbath has nothing to do with the original creation of the earth or the creation of angels. It was given for man to honor His Creator for all the work He did in those six days!

The YECs also teach that those who believe in the Gap Theory are wrong because they see the possibility of prehistoric men living on the earth prior to it becoming without form and void. The YECs state this violates Adam being the first man: *"The first man Adam was made a living soul; the last Adam was made a quickening spirit"* (1 Corinthians 15:45). No person who accepts the Gap Theory believes that prehistoric man-like creatures came from Adam! Tests that have been made on the DNA of so-called prehistoric man have shown there is no relationship with modern man.[62] Adam was the first man made in the image of God and Jesus came to earth as a member of that race of man.

The YECs make another false assertion against the Gap Theorists by claiming they believe we are now living on the second earth.

> Why does Revelation 21:1 state that the earth we live on now is the "first" earth if it really is not?[63]

No one who believes in the Gap Theory believes we are living on the second earth! The first earth was created according to Genesis 1:1, became without form and void in Genesis 1:2, and made new again in Genesis 1:3-31. We are living on that same first earth that will one day be destroyed by fire (2 Peter 3:10-13).

Most of the YECs also use two verses found in the Gospels in an effort to prove that all of creation occurred at the same time just a few thousand years ago. The verses are found in the text concerning the time when the Pharisees tempted Jesus by asking Him questions concerning divorce.

> *"The Pharisees also came unto him, tempting him, and saying unto him, Is it lawful for a man to put away his wife for every cause? And he answered and said unto them, Have ye not read, that he which <u>made them at the beginning</u> made them male and female. And said, For this cause shall a man leave father and mother, and shall cleave to his wife: and they twain shall be one flesh?"* (Matthew 19:3-5) (Emphasis mine)

> *"And they said, Moses suffered to write a bill of divorcement, and to put her away. And Jesus answered and said unto them, For the hardness of your heart he wrote you this precept. But <u>from the beginning of the creation</u> God made them male and female. For this cause shall a man leave his father and mother, and cleave to his wife;*

And they twain shall be one flesh: so then they are no more twain, but one flesh." (Mark 10:4-8) (Emphasis mine)

It is the assertion of the YECs that the underlined phrases *"made them at the beginning"* in Matthew and *"from the beginning of the creation"* in Mark proves that Adam and Eve were created at the very same time as the heaven and the earth since the words *"in the beginning"* are found in Genesis 1:1.

In each text, Jesus replied by reminding the Pharisees of the law of marriage that God had given to Adam and Eve: *"Therefore shall a man leave his father and his mother, and shall cleave unto his wife: and they shall be one flesh"* (Genesis 2:24). It is evident that Jesus was not referring to the beginning of the creation of the heaven and earth, but to the beginning of the human race when God created Adam and Eve and established the institution of marriage! To imply that these verses are teaching that Adam and Eve were created at the same time as the heaven and earth is a gross misrepresentation and misuse of Scripture!

These are the primary verses that are used by the YECs to try to disprove the beliefs of those who hold to the Gap Theory. It has been clearly shown that all their accusations are without merit. If there were flaws in the belief that there is a gap of time between the first two verses of the Bible, some substantive reason to refute it would have been found by now. It has not! Those who oppose the Gap Theory have failed badly in their attempts to discredit it.

Scientific Misinformation Used by The YECs

The YECs not only misuse Scripture in their efforts to prove that the earth is very young, but they also attempt to use scientific information. Much of what they present as science, however, is more erroneous than their interpretations of Scripture. Kent Hovind of CSE has traveled all over the United States teaching about his belief in a young earth. He also sells videos that have been used in many churches and schools that use both the Bible and science to try to prove that the earth is not very old.

One of his videos, entitled *"The Age of The Earth"*, supposedly proves that the earth could not be millions or billions of years old. He introduces himself as Dr. Kent Hovind and states that he taught High School Science for 15 years before beginning CSE. There are many things that he teaches on this video that are scientifically flawed, but I will limit my remarks to what he taught about the rotation of the earth and the orbit of the moon.

In the video, Hovind states that the moon is getting farther from the earth. He then contends that the altitude of the moon above the earth proves that it could not have been rotating around the earth for billions of years getting farther away every year. The following is a transcript taken directly from his video.

> The moon is going around the earth. How many knew that? That the moon goes around the earth? Did you know as the moon goes around it is getting farther away? We are slowly losing the moon. It's only a few inches a year, no big deal, nothing to worry about. Plus, there's nothing you can do about it anyway. But the moon is getting farther from the earth every year. Now, kids this is going to be complicated so listen carefully. The moon is getting farther from the earth every year – so that means it used to be closer! How many of

you can figure that out with no help at all? If you run all the math on this, you will find out that 1.2 billion years ago the moon was whizzing around just above the earth's surface. That explains what happened to the tall dinosaurs – they got MOONED! You can't say it is 4.6 billion years old – it is just geo-physically impossible!

At the end of this dissertation the screen presents a picture of the moon just above the earth's surface hitting dinosaurs on the head. Of course everyone laughs, but they have just been given false information and they don't even know it! What is the real truth about the altitude of the moon's orbit?

If it is true that the moon is getting farther away at this point in time, who knows what it was doing one hundred years ago. His supposed proof totally removes God out of the equation! The law of equilibrium teaches that the God Who created all things also keeps things as they were created. It is very similar to global warming and cooling. The earth goes through a period of time when it is warmer and the ice caps start melting. Then it goes through a colder time when it starts freezing again. The earth is under His control and so is the orbit of the moon!

If Hovind is a true scientist, then he should know that if the moon is getting farther from the earth then its orbital speed will have to be slowing down. The distance that it has to travel to make one revolution around the earth is farther since the radius from the center of the earth is being increased. If it is traveling farther at a slower speed then the time it takes for one orbit will be drastically increasing. Yet, the moon remains on its approximate orbital period of 28 days just as it always has.

The Jewish calendar is based on the moon's orbital period and it has never changed.

If the orbital period was changing then the revolution of the moon on its axis would also have to change at the very same rate. The orbital period of the moon and the rotation about its axis are exactly the same resulting in the same face of the moon always pointing towards the earth. If one has changed, then the other must also change!

On the same video, Hovind teaches that the rotation of the earth is slowing down. He uses his Power Point presentation to present the following dates when a second was added to the clock.

January 1973	January 1974	January 1975
January 1976	January 1977	January 1978
January 1979	January 1980	July 1981
July 1982	July 1983	July 1985
January 1988	January 1990	January 1991
July 1992	July 1993	July 1994
January 1996		

With these dates before the group he was teaching, the following transcript presents his words.

> The earth is spinning about 1,000 miles per hour at the equator. The earth is slowing down! The earth slows down enough that every once in a while they have to add a tick to the clock to put it back on schedule. The earth slows down a thousandth of a second every day. June 1992 was one second longer because it had a leap second. Most people have heard of leap years, but most people have never heard of a leap second even though we have one every year or year and a half. We have to

have one because the earth is slowing down and we have to put the clocks back on schedule. Now, kids this is going to be complicated so listen carefully! The earth is spinning but it's slowing down. Which means it used to be going FASTER! How many can figure that out? Now if you go back a few billion years, the earth was spinning real fast! You think the dinosaurs lived 200 million years ago. I know what happened to them!

At this point, his presentation shows the earth spinning like a top with dinosaurs flying off into space. Once again, everyone laughed, but they had again been given false information!

The same principle holds true here that was mentioned concerning the moon's orbit. The rotational speed of the earth is always under God's control! If He needs to speed it up a little, or slow it down, to keep it as He created it to be, He is able to do it. Anyone who looks at what the earth's rotation is doing at one point in time and assumes that it has always had the same movement has removed God from consideration! But, this is not the most serious problem with Hovind's use of the rotation of the earth to try to prove that it is only a few thousand years old.

He uses the dates when a second was added to try to prove the earth is slowing down, but they have nothing to do with the earth slowing down! The rotation of the earth about its axis is almost exactly 24 hours of 60 minute hours and 60 second minutes. Almost, but not exactly! Therefore, every year or year and a half a second is added as an adjustment to keep the clock correct. If the leap second is added because the earth is slowing down, you would have to add one second after one year, two seconds after two years, three seconds after three years, etc. The leap second is only an adjustment and has nothing to do with the rotation of the earth slowing down! Surely, any scientist or mathematician would know this. But, even this is not the most egregious error in his charge that the earth's rotation is slowing down.

If the earth is really rotating slower than the clock, then the clock would be slightly ahead of the position of the earth after each rotation. The rotation of the earth cannot be changed so the clock is adjusted from time to time to keep the times consistent. If the earth is going slower, a second would have to be SUBTRACTED from the clock, not ADDED to it, to adjust the clock back to the location of the earth! However, a leap second is added to the clock from time to time because one rotation of the earth takes slightly longer than 24 hours.

The two examples given of the scientific presentations given by Hovind on the video is typical of other examples in his entire presentation. His lessons are laced with humor that causes people to laugh instead of think. He even pointed out on the video that the word 'muse' means to think and the negative prefix 'a' in front of it gives the word 'amuse' which means not to think. Those who watch his videos or listen to him speak will be entertained but they will not be enlightened about the age of the earth!

❧

Does it really matter if these young earth organizations are presenting false science and wrong interpretations of Scripture as long as they are making people believe that God is the Creator and evolution is wrong? Anyone who stands to teach and preach for Jesus Christ needs to be totally devoted to speaking the truth. *"But if I tarry long, that thou mayest know how thou oughtest to behave thyself in the house of God, which is the church of the living God, the pillar and ground of the truth"* (1 Timothy 3:15). If the church is to be the pillar and ground of the truth, then any school or organization that is based on Christianity should also be devoted to that principle! Whether it is an interpretation of Scripture or a presentation of science, the truth must prevail!

It does not really matter if YECs build a playground with dinosaurs in it or huge museums that have gardens with a robotic man and woman standing by a dinosaur. That is no proof that dinosaurs were in the Garden of Eden or on Noah's ark! The YECs are making a mistake by teaching a false theory about a young earth. The accurate uses of Scripture and science cannot be used to prove a false theory. Make no mistake - their entire ministries are based on this false belief.

The reputation of Christianity has been tarnished by many of the televangelists who have dishonestly used their ministries for financial gain and personal prosperity. These multi-million dollar ministries that teach about a young earth will also do harm as more people begin to investigate what they are teaching. As the absurdity of many of their scientific claims and their gross misuse of Scripture is revealed, people will even begin to doubt what they teach against evolution and may also doubt their teaching that God is the Creator of all things. It is frightening to think of what may happen to young people who grow up being taught this false theory when they find out that what they were told about the earth being a few thousand years old was all wrong! Will it cause them to assume that everything else in the Bible is wrong also?

This information has been provided to answer the attacks and charges made by those who believe the earth is very young against those who believe that a gap of time exists between the first two verses of the Bible, allowing for the earth to be very old. I have tried to be fair and complete in presenting their dissenting views using the referenced materials. In all of the opposition against the Gap Theory, not a single charge can be legitimately substantiated, or be shown to have any validity.

YECs believe the Gap Theory was developed because of the geological findings that show the earth to be very old. Thus, it is their contention that science gave birth to the theory and not Scripture. Evidence has been shown that people believed in the Gap Theory for hundreds of years before geologists made their discoveries! Their discoveries only validated the belief of the theologians who believed in the Gap Theory.

YECs try to refute the many verses used by the Gap Theorists that show that the original earth was not created without form and void, but that it became that way as a result of God's judgment following the sin of Lucifer. Then they try to find scriptures that will prove that there could be no death on earth before Adam sinned, and that the six days work was the very beginning of God's creation. They have failed in both of these areas.

YECs also present a lot of false scientific information in an effort to prove that real scientists are wrong. Well, real scientists are wrong when they try to teach evolution or deny any of

God's creative acts, but the Christian can counter their teachings with the truth! God's Word is true and He doesn't need falsehoods to prove it!

The best evidence given by the YECs in an effort to prove that the earth is only a few thousand years old is very flimsy, and their attacks against those who believe in the Gap Theory are baseless. If there had been better reasons to condemn the Gap Theory, surely they would have been used. The critics have been answered and the Gap Theory stands as the most likely account of how God brought His creation into being.

True science proves that the earth and life on it could only have come into existence by the power of a Supreme Being. Our eternal God is not only Creator, but He is also the greatest Scientist! He has always existed so it should not be a surprise that He has been very busy in His creation for millions or billions of years. The life that existed on earth prior to it becoming without form and void was created by Him and then destroyed by His judgment. The earth that now is and the life that is on it are also testimonies of His greatness and power!

Chapter 7
THE WONDER OF IT ALL

In the beginning God created the heaven and the earth. With such a simple proclamation, God opened His divine Scripture to men. It is a simple, yet very profound statement! He didn't try to prove His existence or describe His own beginning. As the eternal God, He had no beginning (Psalm 90:2). He just tells us what He did in the beginning. Many minds have been filled with wonder as this verse has been contemplated.

The word 'wonder' is one that adequately describes the reaction of man in considering God's great work of creation. When used as a noun, it means to be filled with awe, admiration, and astonishment. When used as a verb, it describes a person being filled with doubt, curiosity, and many questions. When we consider the greatness of His creation, we are surely filled with wonder and that creates a lot of wondering on our part. Questions like "How?", "When?", and "Why?" can easily come to mind. No person should ask "Who?" because it is readily apparent that only God can create.

The life, ministry, and teaching of Jesus also filled people with wonder. Many were amazed as they heard Him teach:

"And all bare him witness, and wondered at the gracious words which proceeded out of his mouth. And they said, Is not this Joseph's son?" (Luke 4:22). His own disciples were amazed at the power He displayed over creation: *"And he said unto them, Where is your faith? And they being afraid wondered, saying one to another, What manner of man is this! for he commandeth even the winds and water, and they obey him"* (Luke 8:25). After the birth of Jesus, the shepherds went forth telling others what they had seen and heard on that night (Luke 2:11-17). Many who heard them were filled with wonder and even Mary had many questions in her own heart. *"And all they that heard it wondered at those things which were told them by the shepherds. But Mary kept all these things, and pondered them in her heart."* (Luke 2:18, 19). As men have wondered about the person of Jesus Christ, so have they been filled with wonder concerning His creation.

There are two groups of individuals who have accomplished great things for mankind because they were filled with wonder – those who have been inventors and those who have made great discoveries. There is an old adage that states, "Necessity is the mother of invention." This simply means that a need caused someone to come up with a solution that would satisfy that need. The inventor came up with an idea because he wondered if something could be done in a faster, cheaper, better, or safer way. The greatest discoveries were made by individuals, however, who found something that had been done by God.

Man has always admired the creation of God since the first time Adam looked up and wondered at the beauty of the heavens: *"The heavens declare the glory of God; and the firmament showeth his handywork"* (Psalm 19:1). The beauty that Adam observed has caused many others to be filled with questions as they sought to understand why such a great God would be concerned with finite man. *"When I consider thy heavens, the work of thy fingers, the moon and the stars, which thou hast ordained; What is man, that thou art mindful of him? and the son of man, that thou visitest him?"* (Psalm 8:3, 4). While the heavens and many things on Earth were observed from the beginning, many other discoveries have been made through the ages that have filled the discoverer with wonder.

All who have visited Niagara Falls on the New York and Canadian border have been filled with awe at the tremendous sight and sound of the cascading waters. Even though they may have traveled a great distance and were fully expecting to see something great, they were still overcome by the awesomeness and majesty of it all. Can you imagine the first settler who was out exploring and followed the sound as it grew louder and louder until he stood on the bank? Or, can you imagine the surprise of the ones who were traveling west and suddenly walked up on the edge of the Grand Canyon and gazed across the vast expanse of that colorful scene for the first time? There are literally thousands of other scenes that would cause the ones who discovered them to be overcome with awe and exclaim, "Oh, Lord! Now we see what only Your hands could have done!"

One of the most outstanding things found in God's creation is the human body. It is absolutely amazing and unbelievable that so many people consider it to be a work of chance or an accident. The only way that anyone could study the human body and believe that it exists because of evolution is because they have deliberately removed from their minds any possibility that God is the Creator of all things. According to the scriptures, when God is not given consideration as the source of all things a person becomes a fool and reaches many foolish conclusions: *"The fool hath said in his heart, There is no God"* (Psalm 14:1a) and *"Because that, when they knew God, they glorified him not as God, neither were thankful; but became vain in their imaginations, and their foolish heart was darkened. Professing themselves to be wise, they became fools"* (Romans 1:21, 22).

Many discoveries are still being made today concerning the intricacies and complexities that are found in the human body. The many functions of the various organs and how certain chemicals are produced by one part of the body to meet the needs of another part are absolutely amazing. Just one cell is too magnificent to have just happened by accident, yet the human body is made up of millions of these cells! The Psalmist David did not know as much about his body as we know about ours, yet he was overwhelmed with the thought of what God had done when He made him as he attested in Scripture.

> *"I will praise thee; for I am fearfully and wonderfully made: marvellous are thy works; and that my soul knoweth right well. My substance was not hid from thee, when I was made in secret, and curiously wrought in the lowest parts of the earth. Thine eyes did see my substance, yet being unperfect; and in thy book all my members were written, which in continuance were fashioned, when as yet there was none of them. How precious also are thy thoughts unto me, O God! how great is the sum of them!"* (Psalm 139:14-17).

Have you ever stopped to think about what a person must ignore to believe in evolution? Just consider the eyes and how they work with their optic nerves transferring what enters the pupil of the eye to the brain. Consider a tiny baby being born with every tiny blood vessel and artery connected just perfectly. To believe that the first human evolved from a lower life form is to believe that it had to happen twice at the same time. If only one had evolved it would have died and that would have been the end of it. But, evolution must believe that a male and a female evolved at the very same time so they would be able to produce after their own kind. It takes faith to believe that God was the Creator of Adam and Eve and it takes ignorance to believe in evolution. Ignorance comes from the word 'ignore' and the evolutionist has to ignore too many things to believe as he does!

To accept God as Creator should cause us to be filled with wonder, but we should also be amazed at what He has provided for us. From the beginning, men knew that God not only provided water, air, and food for their life-giving sustenance, but many other things as well. It has been found that certain herbs, roots, leaves, and plants have properties that are available to heal the body when it is sick. When we accept God as our Creator and discover how He has gloriously provided for our care, we should lift our eyes to the heavens and declare, "Oh, Lord! Now I know how You have provided for us!"

Thus far, the wonder associated with God's creation of the Earth and mankind has been presented. It was necessary that these things be discussed before we started looking at some of the greatest discoveries made by man. It is not just the fact that

God created all things, but He established physical laws and put them in place to control His creation. The Bible declares that He created all things and that all things would continue to exist because of His power. *"For by him were all things created, that are in heaven, and that are in earth, visible and invisible, whether they be thrones, or dominions, or principalities, or powers: all things were created by him, and for him: And he is before all things, and by him all things consist"* (Colossians 1:16, 17).

God gave many laws to His people Israel through His servant Moses. Some of them were social laws concerning how the people were to treat one another and how the nation was to be judged. There were ceremonial and sacrificial laws that were to guide the worship of their God. The Ten Commandments were given on tables of stone and were commonly called the laws of God. There have been many times when man failed to keep these laws as God had commanded them. But, God established physical laws that would control His creation and man is totally unable to break those laws!

There are two sets of physical laws (or laws of physics) that will be discussed here. The first will be the laws of thermodynamics and the second will be the laws that concern gravity and motion. Someone said, "Many people have tried to break the law of gravity, but they have all been broken by it!" These laws were established by God and have been discovered by physicists and scientists, and we are all forced to live under their influences. Hopefully, our study will help us to wonder at it all!

The science of thermodynamics deals with the relationships that exist between heat and other forms of energy, especially mechanical energy. There are two laws of thermodynamics that have been established by a large amount of scientific evidence. There are no known exceptions to their validity. These two laws will be presented here and we will see how they relate to our study of creation.

The first law of thermodynamics states: "In a closed system, the total amount of energy is constant."[64] When God created the solar system, it contained all the energy and matter that we would ever need. Man cannot create nor destroy energy, but energy can be changed from one form to another. We cannot destroy matter either! Energy and matter are actually equivalent as Einstein proved with his equation $e = mc^2$. Matter is made up of atoms. A pile of wood may be burned and all that is left to our view will be a pile of ashes, but all the atoms still remain. The thermal energy that comes from the fire goes into the atmosphere as the carbon in CO_2 and hydrogen in water. The energy remains, though it changes from one form of energy to another. The ashes go back into the ground and even add nutrients for future growth.

The second law of thermodynamics states: "It is impossible in principle to construct an engine, operating in a cycle that will produce mechanical work by extracting heat from a single reservoir and not return any heat to a reservoir at a lower temperature."[65] This law has been stated another way, "It is impossible for any self-acting machine, unaided by any external agent, to convey heat from one body to another at a higher temperature."[66] One thing that is taught by this law is the fact that a machine cannot convert as much energy as it uses. In other words, a gas generator can use gasoline to generate electricity but it consumes more energy in gasoline than it can generate in electricity. Some of the energy from the gasoline will go into the heat that is dispelled from the engine. This law states that there will never be a perpetual motion machine – a machine that generates enough energy to operate itself without any outside help.

Now, what does all this mean? It means we are totally dependent on God! He has provided energy for us through wind, oil, coal, nuclear power and many other fuel agents. As we use energy, He is able to recycle it through His creation. With all the discoveries that man has made about thermodynamics, there is surely so much more that God is doing that has not yet been discovered. Yet, we marvel at it all! Truly, God does all things well!

Our study of the law of gravity requires that we first of all become acquainted with Sir Isaac Newton (1642-1727). He was born at Woolsthorpe, Lincolnshire, in England on December 25, 1642. As a child, he wanted to play with mechanical devices instead of studying. He entered Trinity College, Cambridge University, in 1661. He was not an exceptional student and graduated in 1665 without any special distinctions. After his graduation, over a period of eighteen months (1665-67) he made three great discoveries.

He established the science of spectrum analysis that deals with light and colors. He discovered that sunlight is a mixture of light of all colors. He caused a beam of sunlight to pass through a prism that divided the light into the various colors of the rainbow. He determined that apples appear red because there is red in the light from the sun and without that color being present the apples would not appear as red. In

1969 I purchased a 35 mm camera with a strobe light. We had a church with green carpet and when pictures were taken in the building the carpet appeared a dull brown. I never understood why until I read what Newton had discovered about light. My strobe had a white light that did not contain the color green, therefore, the pictures could not reflect green. Newton published the results of these experiments in *Opticks* in 1704.

His second discovery was the branch of mathematics known as calculus. There are two primary branches of calculus – differential and integral. Differential calculus helps determine the rate of change while integral is used to determine summations.

His third discovery dealt with the theory of motion and gravitation. A tale has been repeated often that an apple fell on his head causing him to determine the law of gravitation, but this is evidently not true. He was drinking tea in his garden and wondering about what kept the moon in orbit over the earth when an apple fell from a nearby tree. He was suddenly overcome with the belief that the same force that caused the apple to fall was also keeping the moon in orbit.

He began experiments that proved that all the planets were kept in orbit about the sun by the sun's gravitational force, and the moon was kept in orbit around the earth by earth's gravitational pull. He proved that the moon is falling just like the apple, but because the moon is moving at the right speed, its fall keeps it in a circle above the earth at the same altitude. He said that if the moon was not falling it would continue in a straight line and go away from the earth.

Newton gave the results of his studies and observations in the form of three laws of motion that became the foundation for physics:

1. An object at rest remains at rest, and an object in motion continues in motion with constant velocity (that is, constant speed in a straight line) unless the object experiences a net external force.

2. The acceleration of an object is directly proportional to the net external force acting on the object and inversely proportional to the object's mass.

3. To every action there is always an equal and opposite reaction.

These laws were discovered by Newton but they were established by God to hold His creation together. These are the very laws that keep our satellites in orbit around the earth today.

While Newton was still a young man, he discovered a study that was more fascinating to him than his scientific studies – the study of theology. While he did teach at a university and published some of his findings, he spent the majority of his time studying about God. I believe most people fit in one of three groups. Some are like us, just of average intelligence, but by faith we believe in God and are convinced that He is the Creator and controller of all things. Others are like us, just of average intelligence, but they consider themselves to be too intelligent to believe in God so they come to foolish conclusions about evolution and atheism. Others, like Sir Isaac Newton, are of superior intelligence. They are so intelligent they see God's fingerprints in everything! When great thinkers such as Sir Isaac Newton and others have discovered the laws of God that control light and colors, thermodynamics, gravity, and the laws of motion and many more great truths, then they will have the greatest thought as they say, "Oh, Lord! Now I know what You were thinking!"

While Newton was an excellent scientist, mathematician, and astrologer, he did have some shortcomings in his doctrines. He held to the Arian belief that denies the Trinity. He believed that Jesus was less than God. He used verses where Jesus stated, "He had come to do the Father's will", and that, "His Father was greater than all", to justify his beliefs. He ignored the fact that Jesus was speaking as One dwelling in the flesh when He made these statements. He did have a strong belief that God was the Creator of all things, and this surely intensified his efforts to know more about the One who filled him with wonder. This should also be true for us.

As stated earlier, when men have looked upon God's creation, they have been filled with wonder that led to a lot of wondering. This led to many questions. The answers that have been discovered for the many questions have only increased the original awe, admiration and astonishment that the observer had in the beginning. What really stands out even more than the fascination of creation is the faithfulness of God, as we understand how the One who created all things continues to control them through the physical laws that He has established. It is the constancy and the consistency of God that causes us to go from the "wonder of it all" to "wonder not at all". In other words, there are some things we no longer wonder about because we know about the faithfulness of God.

On the fifth day of creation, the Bible states:

"And God said, Let the waters bring forth abundantly the moving creature that hath life, and fowl that may fly above the earth in the open firmament of heaven. And God created great whales, and every living creature that moveth, which the waters brought forth abundantly, after their kind, and every winged fowl after his kind: and God saw that it was good. And God blessed them, saying, Be fruitful, and multiply, and fill the waters in the seas, and let fowl multiply in the earth" (Genesis 1:20-22).

On the beginning of the sixth day:

"And God said, Let the earth bring forth the living creature after his kind, cattle, and creeping thing, and beast of the earth after his kind: and it was so. And God made the beast of the earth after his kind, and cattle after their kind, and every thing that creepeth upon the earth after his kind: and God saw that it was good" (Genesis 1:24, 25).

Therefore, when we see two cardinals making a nest in our backyard, we know they are only obeying God. As the eggs are laid and the time comes when they are to crack open, we do not wonder about what the little birds will be. We know they will be "after their kind."

In like manner, from the little hummingbird to the majestic eagle, each one continues in perfection after its own kind. In the water, it may be a tiny minnow or a great whale, but each one is perfect in its own way. On earth, the tiniest creature and the largest animal are only continuing to be what God created and commanded them to be. We do not wonder what their offspring will be! Each one will be after its own kind.

After a long night, we do not wonder if the sun will come up in the morning - we just wait for the first rays of sunlight. There are tables already prepared that provide the exact times of sunrise and sunset on every day for many years in advance. Our tides are affected by the gravitational pull of the moon. Therefore, the low and high tides are determined by the location of the moon. You do not have to wonder when high tide will be on a particular day many years from now. God has established the laws of motion that control the orbit of the moon and the rotation of the earth and there is no chance of them changing.

When you place a hammer on a table, you do not have to wonder if it will be there when you return. Newton's first law states that "every body continues in a state of rest" unless some force moves it. If no other force acts on that hammer, it will be there! If you hold up that hammer and drop it, you will not have to wonder if it will fall. The law of gravity demands that it will. These are God's laws! Newton just happened to be the human who discovered them and explained them so we could all understand.

If you use glue to stick something to the wall or ceiling, you may have to watch it for a while to see if it will stay. But, when a satellite is placed into orbit the scientist does not have to wonder and wait to see if it will remain in orbit, as long as it has the right parameters. The laws of motion demand that it will stay in orbit until some other force affects its velocity or direction of motion.

The greatness of God's creation caused man to do a lot of wondering. As we have learned more about His creation, we have also learned more about Him. The glory of creation is great but it pales in comparison to the glory of God. We should never be so fascinated with what has been made, that we lose sight of the faithfulness of the One who made all things.

The astronauts who traveled to the moon and back were blessed to have viewed the earth in a way that we can only see in pictures. The astronauts were not just good pilots, but they were brilliant scientists and engineers as well. Captain Eugene Cernan made two flights to the moon – Apollo 10 and Apollo 17. He was one of the astronauts featured in the film *"In The Shadow Of The Moon"* and shared this testimony of viewing the earth on his return back home.

> "I felt that I was standing on a plateau out there in space. A plateau that science and technology had allowed me to get to. But, now what I was seeing, and even more importantly what I was feeling at that time, science and technology had no answers for. Literally, no answers for, because there I was and there you are – the earth, dynamic and overwhelming. And I felt that the earth had too much purpose and logic and was too beautiful to have just happened by accident. There has to be Somebody bigger than you and bigger than me! And, I mean this in a spiritual sense, not a religious sense. There has to be a Creator of the universe above the religions we create to govern our lives."

The beauty of the earth evidently caused him to be filled with wonder, but he did not wonder about how it came into being.

❦

There are some things about God that you do not have to wonder about at all! You do not have to wonder whether or not God loves you! You do not have to wonder if Jesus died for you on the cross of Calvary. *"But we see Jesus, who was made a little lower than the angels for the suffering of death, crowned with glory and honour; that he by the grace of God should taste death for every man"* (Hebrews 2:9). If you do not know Jesus Christ as your personal Savior, you can repent of your sins and place your faith in Him by calling on His name right now. *"For whosoever shall call upon the name of the Lord shall be saved"* (Romans 10:13).

The wonder of it all is you will not have to wonder at all. Jesus has promised to make of you a new creature: *"Therefore if any man be in Christ, he is a new creature: old things are passed away; behold, all things are become new"* (2 Corinthians 5:17). He will give you the indwelling Holy Spirit to let you know that He has kept His promise: *"Hereby know we that we dwell in him, and he in us, because he hath given us of his Spirit"* (1 John 4:13).

God uses the story of His creation to draw people to Himself. Those who deny His creation are in fact denying Him. As His new creation, you can be one who can lead others to accept our Savior. As the Psalmist said that the heavens declare the glory of God, it is now your job to shine forth His glory as well. *"Let your light so shine before men, that they may see your good works, and glorify your Father which is in heaven"* (Matthew 5:16).

Brigadier General Charlie Duke was another of the astronauts who was featured in the film mentioned above. He flew to the moon on Apollo 16. He shared this personal testimony at the conclusion of the film.

> "A friend of ours got us to go to a Bible study at a tennis club. After that weekend, I said to Jesus, 'I give You my life and if You are real come into my life.' He did and I had a sense of peace that was hard to describe. It was so dramatic we started sharing our story. I would say that my walk on the moon lasted for three days and it was a great adventure, but my walk with God will last forever."

He knew the joy of being on a journey that goes all the way to Heaven, not just to the moon. You can join him on that journey and you will know the wonder of it all!

Chapter 8
LIVING BY THE LAW

There is a vast difference in theory and truth. Sometimes, things that once were only theories are proven to be facts. At other times, certain conditions and circumstances must exist for a theory or theories to be true. There are also major differences in the things that are considered facts and those which are considered as laws. Something may be a fact at a certain point in time, but at a later time and place it can no longer stand the test of trustworthiness. Any law that has been established will always be true regardless of the changing of conditions.

Sir Isaac Newton's observations led him to form theories about gravity and the laws of motion. Further investigations by Newton proved those theories are not only true, but are also laws that cannot be broken. Now, after several hundred years, many other scientists have validated that all men must live under the constraints of the physical laws that God has established.

The Bible is clear in teaching that no person (other than Jesus) will be able to live the moral law of God to perfection.

All who break the spiritual laws of God will be broken by those same laws: *"For as many as have sinned without law shall also perish without law: and as many as have sinned in the law shall be judged by the law"* (Romans 2:12). Physics is clear that everyone must live by the physical laws that God has established to rule the universe. Therefore, it is incumbent that we be acquainted with these physical laws.

It is foolish for anyone to have a theory that opposes the established laws of God. The scientist who has theorized that an accidental physical occurrence has brought the earth and its system of equilibrium into existence by chance has ignored the very laws of God that he knows to be true. Another part of the second law of thermodynamics that was introduced in the previous chapter states: "In thermodynamics, a system left to itself tends to go from a state with a very ordered set of energies (one that has only a small probability of being randomly formed) to one in which there is less order (or that has a high probability of being randomly formed.)"[67] This simply states that any system left to itself will become more disorganized, not organized! The earth system is very organized.

Plants breathe in carbon dioxide and give off oxygen. Living beings breathe in oxygen and give off carbon dioxide. They each provide what the other needs. Water is drawn from the surface of the earth into the atmosphere and then it returns to the earth in the form of rain. The earth system remains very organized regardless of all that happens on it. The second law of thermodynamics states it should become less organized unless some other force is acting on it. The theory that the earth came about because of an accident and continues under its own power will always be only a theory because it is against the known laws of God.

The most common theories about an accidental beginning of the universe and solar system, however, may not necessarily be against the laws of thermodynamics. Still, that does not mean that those theories are necessarily true. The Big Bang Theory (BBT) is the most prominent belief of how the universe came into being. The Nebular hypothesis is the primary theory of how the solar system came into being with the sun, its planets, and all their moons.

In the early 1900s, there were two basic beliefs concerning the conditions that exist in the universe. Some believed in the "Solid State Theory" of the universe, whereby all the galaxies were believed to be in the places where they have always been and will always be. Albert Einstein agreed with this view.[68] There were others who believed that the universe was constantly expanding with movement in all the galaxies. There was great disagreement until a discovery was made in 1927.

Dr. Edwin Hubble (1889-1953) used a 100 inch telescope to study the galaxies from Mount Wilson Observatory and observed that all galaxies were moving away from earth at a high rate of speed.[69] NASA's Hubble Telescope was named in his honor. After his discovery, most astronomers started believing in an expanding universe. This group included Dr. Einstein who changed his beliefs. There were some, however, who would not be persuaded.

Fred Hoyle was a British astronomer who persisted in believing in the "Solid State Theory". He was making a broadcast on the British Broadcasting Company in 1950 when he ridiculed the people who disagreed with him by stating that they believed a "Big Bang" had caused the origin of the universe.[70] Thus, the name "Big Bang" was given to this theory by someone who did not even believe in it! Most of the people who believe in what we now refer to as "Big Bang" do not believe there was an explosion but rather an expansion. Just what do the "Big Bang Theory" people believe?

They believe the universe came into existence as a "singularity". A singularity is a zone that defies anything we know about physics or astronomy. It is something that happened one time and cannot be duplicated. They believe that our universe began as an infinitesimally small, infinitely hot and infinitely dense, something.[71] They do not know where it came from or why it appeared. They state that it apparently inflated (the "Big Bang"), expanded and cooled, going from very, very small and very, very hot, to the size and temperature of the current universe. They believe that in the first three seconds it went from very small to very large and has continued to expand. The distance to the individual stars and the rate at which they are moving away from us causes the astronomers to date the time of this event at over 13 billion years ago.

The very significant thing about the BBT's belief is the fact that they believe from their discoveries and observations that the universe had a beginning! They believe that there was nothing prior to that singularity and time and space began at its occurrence. Their discoveries further prove what the Bible says, *"In the beginning, God created"* (Genesis 1:1).

Did God use a singularity to bring about the universe? Absolutely! It cannot be duplicated or explained by natural laws. It must be accepted by faith! It is interesting to note that scientific discoveries do confirm what we believe. When people accept that we are a new creation living on a very old earth, they will not be threatened by what scientists discover but will be thrilled by what they believe.

The Big Bang Theory does not even address the beginning of the solar system. It only deals with the universe. The Nebular hypothesis is the most widely accepted belief explaining the formation of the solar system.[72] It presents the idea that the solar system originated from a rotating nebula (small particles) that cooled and contracted, throwing off rings of matter that contracted into the planets and their moons, while the great mass of the condensing nebula became the sun.[73] Physicists say that this explanation is possible when considering the laws of thermodynamics. From their measurements of radioactive decay, astronomers and physicists believe this occurred over 3 billion years ago, which would be about 10 billion years after the creation of the universe. If these dates are accurate, then the solar system was created and placed in the middle of what was an expanding universe. Yet, there are some things that should be considered that will show the theory is invalid in explaining all the circumstances found in the solar system.

If the rotating nebula contracted into the sun with its various planets spinning off at different altitudes, there would be a similarity in the rotation of the planets with their respective moons. The same natural forces from the spinning would have the same effect on each planet. But, as will be revealed later in this chapter, some moons travel from east to west and others from west to east. One planet even has moons traveling in opposite directions! I challenge anyone to use the laws of physics to explain how this could have occurred. The moons were not placed in their unique orbits around their respective planets by accident or natural phenomena, but by the hand of a creating God!

To really appreciate this, the physical laws that must be satisfied for one body (such as the moon) to be in orbit about another body (such as the earth) must be understood. When an astronaut is observed floating around in his spacecraft many are prone to believe that he is able to do so because there is no gravity at his altitude. That is totally inaccurate! He is floating around because the centrifugal force that is trying to sling him out into space due to the velocity he is traveling is equal to the force of gravity that is trying to pull him back to earth. Thus, the two forces are equal but in opposite directions so he floats around with no resultant force acting on him.

The simple equation used to compute the force of gravity on a body at any altitude is presented here. The following constant values are:

Radius of the earth	$R_F = 20.903 \times 10^6$ feet
Earth's gravitational constant	$\mu = 1.4069 \times 10^{16}$
Nautical mile	$= 6.076.1$ feet

The acceleration due to gravity can be calculated for any altitude by the following equation where R is equal to RE plus the altitude above the earth's surface:

$$\text{Gravity} = \frac{\mu}{R^2} \qquad \text{Equation } 8\text{-}1$$

Using this equation, the gravity on the surface of the earth is 32.2 ft / sec ^{2} and at an altitude of 100 nautical miles it will only decrease to 30.4 ft / sec ^{2}. The same equation can be used to calculate the gravity for any altitude above the moon using the moon's radius and gravitational constant.

To place a satellite in circular orbit, there is one horizontal velocity for each altitude that will create the centrifugal force that will be equal to the force of gravity at that same altitude. The horizontal velocity is perpendicular (90 degrees) to the radius from the center of gravity of the earth and lies in the plane of the desired orbit. The equation to calculate the required velocity at each altitude is:

$$V_C = \sqrt{\frac{\mu}{R}} \qquad \text{Equation } 8-2$$

At an altitude of 100 nautical miles, the horizontal velocity required to insert the satellite into a circular orbit is 25,573.4 ft / sec. Thus, if a vehicle is to be launched into this circular orbit, a computer will guide the vehicle from the launch pad to an altitude of 100 nautical miles and once at that altitude it will continue in the horizontal plane and accelerate until the exact desired velocity is achieved. At that time, the engines are shut off and the vehicle will be in the desired orbit. The centrifugal force from its velocity pointing out towards space is identical to the pull of gravity pointing back towards earth. Newton's first law of motion when converted to such an angular velocity states: "A body rotating with constant angular velocity about a given axis will continue to rotate with the same angular velocity unless acted upon by an unbalanced torque."[74] As the vehicle continues in its circular orbit, the velocity will remain the same and always be in the horizontal plane. It is as if the vehicle is actually falling, but the earth's surface is also falling away at the same rate. If the vehicle is not at the exact appropriate velocity for a circular orbit, the satellite can still be in an elliptical orbit.

While it takes a computer to guide a space vehicle into a desired orbit, God created our solar system by simply saying, "Let it be." He placed nine planets in orbit around the sun (although there may be some doubt about Pluto being a planet). Beginning at the one nearest to the sun and going out, the planets are Mercury, Venus, Earth, Mars, Jupiter, Saturn, Uranus, Neptune, and Pluto. They are all in slightly elliptical orbits and they are all different distances from the sun, yet their velocities around the sun are correct at their respective altitudes for them to remain in orbit.

There are huge differences in the orbits of the various planets. An elliptical orbit has a perigee that is the closest distance and the apogee that is the greatest distance from the body that is being orbited. The perigee of the Earth is 91.4 million miles above the sun and the apogee is 94.5 million miles. On the other hand, Neptune has a perigee of 2.771 billion miles and an apogee of 2.819 billion miles. The orbital period is the time that it takes for a body to make a complete revolution. The period of Earth's orbit, of course, is one year (365 ¼ days). The period of Neptune's orbit is almost 165 years (60,188 days).

God not only placed the planets at the right distances above the sun and traveling at the right speed to keep them in orbit, but He also placed moons in orbit around several of the planets. Mars and Neptune each have two moons traveling in a west to east direction. Uranus has five moons with all of them going in an east to west direction. Saturn has ten moons and one of them (Titan) is about as large as the planet Mercury. Jupiter has twelve moons with eight of them going from west to east and the other four going from east to west. One has to wonder how a scientist could explain how a spinning mass could become a planet that would allow the moons to be going in different directions! The physical explanation is that it is not possible. With God, however, all things are possible!

The Earth has only one moon and it is traveling at about 2300 miles per hour (3312. ft / sec) with a perigee of 221,463 miles and an apogee of 252,710. But, there is something very unique about the moon's orbit and revolution. It takes 365 ¼ days for Earth to make one orbit around the sun and it makes one revolution about its axis every 24 hours. The moon, on the other hand, makes one orbit around Earth every 27 ¹/3 days and it makes one revolution about its axis every 27 ¹/3 days. The moon's orbital period and the time of one revolution are exactly the same! This means that the very same face of the moon always points toward Earth! The only people who have ever seen the other side of the moon are the astronauts who have gone on a lunar mission. It is foolish for anyone to believe that this happened by accident! It has the handprint of God all over it!

His handprint is seen in other things as well. Sometimes an architect or artist has some unique things about their work that would cause a knowledgeable person to recognize their particular work when studied. I once heard one of the astronauts (Col. James Irwin) make the statement that he believed in a Creator because every part of creation carried with it the same design. Every thing is designed with something being in the middle and other objects rotating around it. The planets rotate around the sun and the various moons rotate around their respective planets. Even the smallest part of creation, the atom, is designed after the same pattern.

Everything is made up of atoms. Air, all metals, plastics, paper, water, etc., are all made up of atoms. The atom has a nucleus that is made up of protons or neutrons. Each element has a different number of protons or neutrons making up its nucleus. Each atom has electrons whirling around the nucleus in an orbit very much like a tiny solar system. Their speed, however, is quite different! The electrons complete billions of trips around the nucleus in a millionth of a second!

All atoms are very small, but the hydrogen atom is the smallest of them all. It is so small that a million of them lying side by side will measure less than the thickness of a piece of paper. The very God who designed the solar system has also designed the smallest atom using the same pattern! As the Engineer of all things, it should be no surprise that our unchangeable God would show the consistency of using the same pattern in all things that He did.

When God wanted Moses to build a Tabernacle so that God would have a place to meet with His people, He did not come up with a new design. He used the design of the Tabernacle already in Heaven: *"Who serve unto the example and shadow of heavenly things, as Moses was admonished of God when he was about to make the tabernacle: for, See, saith he, that thou make all things according to the pattern showed to thee in the mount"* (Hebrews 8:5) and *"It was therefore necessary that the patterns of things in the heavens should be purified with these; but the heavenly things themselves with better sacrifices than these"* (Hebrews 9:23).

The Lord established the laws of gravity and motion and then He designed a universe where everything from the smallest to the largest would depend on and obey those laws. The only One who can break those laws is the very One who made them. The law of gravity was broken when an axe head was made to swim. *"But as one was felling a beam, the axe head fell into the water: and he cried, and said, Alas, master! for it was borrowed. And the man of God said, Where fell it? And he showed him the place. And he cut down a stick, and cast it in thither; and the iron did swim"* (2 Kings 6:5, 6). The law of gravity was defied again when Jesus came walking on the water and bid Peter to come to Him.

"And in the fourth watch of the night Jesus went unto them, walking on the sea. And when the disciples saw him walking on the sea, they were troubled, saying, It is a spirit; and they cried out for fear. But straightway Jesus spake unto them, saying, Be of good

cheer; it is I; be not afraid. And Peter answered him and said, Lord, if it be thou, bid me come unto thee on the water. And he said, Come. And when Peter was come down out of the ship, he walked on the water, to go to Jesus. But when he saw the wind boisterous, he was afraid; and beginning to sink, he cried, saying, Lord, save me" (Matthew 14:25-30).

While God has the right and power to change the laws that He has established, we have to learn to live by them and use them for our benefit. The laws of physics that demand the conditions to be satisfied for a satellite to be in orbit have already been presented. His laws must also be followed as a vehicle leaves the launch pad in a powered flight designed to guide that vehicle into a safe orbit.

For many centuries, the laws of motion that were discovered by Sir Isaac Newton have been expressed in equation form. The physicist and mathematician knew what was required to place a man-made satellite into orbit around the earth. The fuels, metals and other materials were not available that would be necessary to build a spacecraft that would be able to insert a satellite into orbit. In recent years, our space agency has not only had the necessary equations, but also the materials to use the laws of God for the betterment of society. We are blessed because scientists have learned to live by and obey the laws of God.

The laws of motion, as presented in the previous chapter, state that a vehicle on a launch pad will remain motionless unless some other force acts upon it. As it sits, the pad is pushing up the exact force that gravity is pulling down. When the engines are ignited, the vehicle begins to move upward if they are producing enough force to overcome the pull of gravity. If the force from the propulsion of the engines is not sufficient to overcome gravity, then the vehicle continues to sit there. The weight experienced by the pad will be less since the force from the engines will also be against the pull of gravity.

The pull of gravity is measured as acceleration. If an object is dropped, it will begin to accelerate towards the ground. For a vehicle to leave the launch pad, the force generated by the engines must create an acceleration that is greater than the effects of gravity. The equation to calculate acceleration is very simple:

$$\text{Acceleration} = \frac{\text{Force}}{\text{Mass}} \qquad \text{Equation 8 - 3}$$

Force represents all the combined forces acting on the vehicle. This includes the forward propulsion from all the engines and the backward aerodynamic drag as the vehicle is going through the atmosphere. Mass is calculated as the weight of the vehicle divided by the measurement of the acceleration of gravity. It should be evident that the acceleration experienced by a vehicle will be increasing as the mass decreases due to fuel being burnt off.

If one knows the flow rate of the fuel, it will be easy to create a graph depicting the acceleration relative to the time of flight. All this reveals, however, is the timeline of the acceleration. It does not reveal the location or speed of the vehicle. Once again, we are indebted to Newton! Around the time that he discovered the laws of motion, he also discovered calculus. Using integral calculus, the velocity and displacement (location) of the vehicle can be calculated for any point in time. The first integral of acceleration provides the velocity and the integral of velocity (second integral of acceleration) presents the location.

It is not sufficient to know the total acceleration of the vehicle. For a vehicle to be guided into an orbit, the engines must develop a force that results in an acceleration that will keep the vehicle in the desired flight path. Therefore, the total force acting on the vehicle has to be broken down into its components. To do this, a three dimensional coordinate system is required. A sample body-fixed coordinate system is presented in Figure 8 – 1.

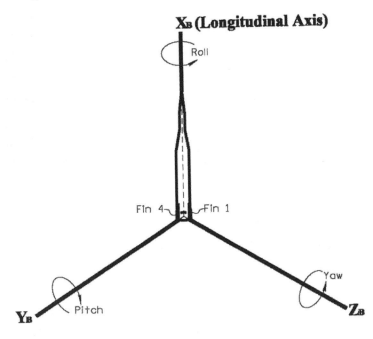

Figure 8 - 1: Body Fixed Coordinate System

In this drawing, the XB axis lies in the longitudinal axis of the vehicle. The ZB axis passes through Fin # 1 and points to the East as the vehicle sits on the launch pad. The YB axis passes through Fin # 4 and is at a 90° angle to XB and ZB. The total force acting on the vehicle from the propulsion of the engines can be expressed in these three components to determine the direction of the resultant acceleration.

When a vehicle only has one engine, it will be centered at the rear and aligned with the longitudinal axis and all its force will be going along the XB axis. To change the direction of the force coming from the engine, it will have actuators that will be used to cause the engine to swivel. Once the engine has swiveled, the direction of the force will change and the total can be expressed by its components along the three axes. Using Equation 8–3, the acceleration along each of the three axes can then be calculated and the effects it is having on the vehicle body can also be determined. The direction that the vehicle body is pointing will change due to the pitch, yaw, and roll angles. A rotation around the XB axis is called the roll of the vehicle. The rotation around the ZB axis is the yaw and around the YB axis is the pitch.

The engines which swivel to change the direction of flight are controlled by two actuators. One actuator is parallel to the YB axis and it will either pull or push on the engine to cause a yaw reaction. The other one is parallel to the ZB axis and causes the vehicle to have a pitch angle. The combined use of these two actuators can also cause a roll about the longitudinal axis.

If a vehicle has more than one engine, the location and alignment of all the engines must be used to determine the total force. When I was last working as an aerospace engineer, the programs used by NASA included the Saturn 1-B and Saturn V vehicles. The Saturn 1-B had a total of eight engines. Four were clustered around the longitudinal axis and were fixed. The other four were spaced around the outside and could swivel to change the direction of flight. The Saturn V had five engines with one fixed and placed in the center. The other four were located on the outside and could swivel. The components of the force of all engines were calculated along the XB, YB, and ZB axes and their sum gave the total force along the three axes. Thus, the acceleration in the three directions was easily calculated along with the corresponding movement of pitch, yaw and roll.

The body fixed coordinate system was necessary to calculate the force and direction acting on the vehicle body, but the system remains with the body as it is moving. There has to be another coordinate system that can be used to calculate the location, velocity and acceleration at any point in time. One of these systems is called the earth fixed coordinate system and is presented in Figure 8 – 2.

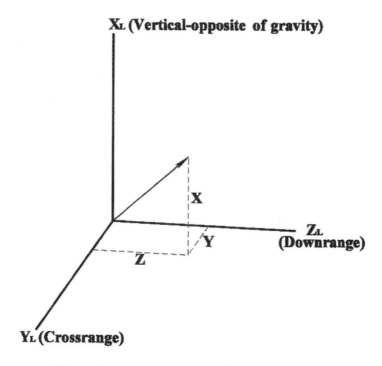

Figure 8 - 2: Earth Fixed Coordinate System

This system has its origin at the launch site. The XL axis is vertical to and opposite of the force of the gravity. The ZL axis is pointing downrange in the direction of the desired flight and YL is to the right at 90°. The XL and ZL axes form the desired flight plane. The ZL and YL axes form the horizontal plane at the launch site. The vector arrow in the drawing simply shows the location of the vehicle and its location is described by its X, Y and Z components. If these parameters are all the information you have, it is described as a three degree of freedom trajectory. But, if you also know the attitude of the vehicle (the direction it is pointing) by the pitch, yaw and roll, then it is called a six degree of freedom trajectory.

Another coordinate system that is essential for the actual flight is the inertial coordinate system that is presented in Figure 8 – 3. This system is identical with the earth fixed coordinate system presented in Figure 8 –2 prior to liftoff of the vehicle. Once the vehicle lifts off the launch pad, however, the inertial coordinate system is frozen as the earth moves beneath it. This coordinate system is needed to guide the actual flight because the acceleration of the vehicle is measured by inertial accelerometers on the vehicle. They do not measure the movement of the earth or the effect of gravity, but only the acceleration that is sensed by the vehicle.

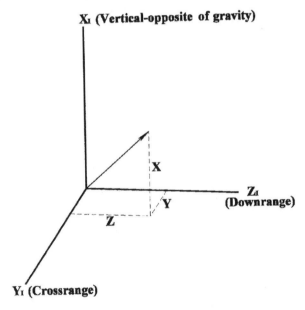

Figure 8 - 3: Inertial Coordinate System

There is one other coordinate system that is important when the satellite has been placed in orbit. It is called the earth centered coordinate system and is shown in Figure 8-4.

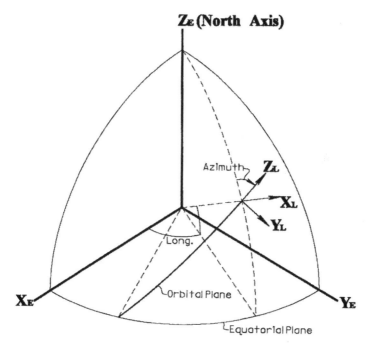

Figure 8 - 4 : Earth Centered Coordinate System

The ZE axis is in the direction of the North Pole along the axis of rotation of the Earth. The XE and YE axes both lie in the equatorial plane. The earth fixed coordinate system is also pictured in Figure 8 – 4 to reveal the relationship between the two systems. The azimuth is the angle of the flight path as measured from the North. The orbital plane and how it intercepts the equatorial plane is also revealed in the drawing.

If the location, velocity and acceleration of the vehicle are known for either the earth fixed, earth centered, or inertial coordinate systems, the same information can easily be calculated and presented in the other coordinate systems as well. The importance of using each of these systems will be revealed in the next chapter where the design of trajectories and orbital maneuvers will be presented.

❦

There are many satellites orbiting the earth. All of them were placed in their respective orbits using the laws of physics that were presented above. In each case, an onboard computer was used to guide the vehicle on a prescribed trajectory to obtain the exact parameters that would assure the desired orbit. The vehicles were man-made, but the laws that were used are God-made! Scientists have only discovered the laws that God used in designing the solar system with all its orbiting planets and moons and used them in our own space program.

In His creation of the universe, God could have used some of His physical laws. However, it should be obvious that more than natural laws were required! He could have performed what is commonly called the "Big Bang" over 13 billion years ago because He certainly existed at that time! Where else could that infinitesimally small and infinitely dense and infinitely hot matter have come from that suddenly started expanding?

He could have decided to place the solar system in the midst of the expanding universe over 3 billion years ago because He was still available and active at that time. Then, He reformed the earth that had become cold and dead and created new beings to live on it just a few thousand years ago.

Any scientist who tries to determine the truth about how this great universe came into existence is making a serious mistake when God is not included in his calculations! Any person who tries to teach from the Bible that God never did any creative work until just a few thousand years ago is also making a serious mistake! We are forced to live according to His physical laws, but He has never been restrained from doing what He wishes.

All the observations and discoveries that have been made about creation seem to show that God did use some of His laws in this great work. But, He obviously did some things that go far beyond natural occurrences so that His personal touch would be seen and recognized. That is why any true discovery should only cause us to be filled with awe and wonder as we glorify Him for the great work He has done!

Chapter 9
A COMMITMENT OF CERTAINTY

It is a wonderful thing when we can undertake a task with absolute certainty that it will be successful. The farmer who plants his seed in the springtime is forced to do his work with a lot of uncertainty about the final fruit of his labors. The quality of the seed he plants and fertilizer that he uses can affect the production of his crop. The weather through the summer months can have a tremendous effect - whether it is too dry, too wet, or too hot. Thus, the farmer undertakes his work with faith that it will be worthwhile, even though there are uncertainties associated with it.

There are some labors, however, that can be done with absolute certainty that they will be successful. These can be in the spiritual or scientific realm and in each case they depend on the faithfulness of God. *"Faithful is he that calleth you, who also will do it"* (1 Thessalonians 5:24). The Christian must be faithful to God's spiritual laws in the service he gives and the scientist must be correct in his use of God's physical laws to receive desired results. Thus, each of them can make a commitment to their respective work with certainty of the outcome.

It is the human who must make a commitment, but it is God Who will bring the desired results to pass: *"Commit thy way unto the LORD; trust also in him; and he shall bring it to pass"* (Psalm 37:5).

The only hope that any lost sinner has for receiving salvation is to come to God in repentance because of his sins as faith is placed in Jesus Christ for His forgiveness. The promise of salvation is certain to all who call on the name of Jesus in this manner: *"For whosoever shall call upon the name of the Lord shall be saved"* (Romans 10:13). One who calls on the name of the Lord is in fact committing his soul into the safe-keeping of the Lord as Paul attested that he had done. *"For the which cause I also suffer these things: nevertheless I am not ashamed: for I know whom I have believed, and am persuaded that he is able to keep that which I have COMMITTED unto him against that day"* (2 Timothy 1:12) (Emphasis mine).

The work of the Christian is both God-ward and man-ward. It is true that not all men will accept our ministries that are offered to them or the messages that we want to share, but some will. God has established some spiritual guidelines, however, that we can follow to be certain that what we do is blessed by God and accepted by more people.

Each Christian is to serve under the Lordship of Jesus Christ! He is the Lord and we are the servants! It is inconsistent to call Jesus "Lord" and then live a life that is not totally dedicated to Him. *"And why call ye me, Lord, Lord, and do not the things which I say?"* (Luke 6:46). When our service is done for the Lord and in His name, we can be certain that much good will come from it. *"And whatsoever ye do in word or deed, do all in the name of the Lord Jesus, giving thanks to God and the Father by him"* (Colossians 3:17).

If we are to serve under the Lordship of Jesus, we must learn to be obedient to His Word. It is good for us to enjoy our church services. It is wonderful when we are fascinated with studying the Bible. Whether we enjoy them or not, however, we are to be doing these things because the Bible commands us to do so. We are told *"Not forsaking the assembling of ourselves together"* (Hebrews 10:25). We are commanded to study the Bible: *"Study to show thyself approved unto God, a workman that needeth not to be ashamed, rightly dividing the word of truth"* (2 Timothy 2:15). In like manner, any thing else we do in obedience to the Word of God will be blessed!

Peter and his fishing friends had toiled all night without any success when Jesus appeared to them on the shore and commanded them to launch out and lower their nets once again. The command didn't make any sense to him, but Peter (also known as Simon) obeyed simply because the Lord had given him the order. *"And Simon answering said unto him, Master, we have toiled all the night, and have taken nothing: nevertheless at thy word I will let down the net"* (Luke 5:5). His obedience caused the nets to be filled with fish. In like manner, we have reason to expect great benefits when we serve in obedience to God's Word and not just because we get personal enjoyment from it.

The motivating force that should be behind our obedience to the Lord and His Word is the power of love – love for God and love for people whom God also loves. It is not enough to only speak the truth to people, but it should also be spoken with love: *"But speaking the truth in love"* (Ephesians 4:15). All the work that we do should be because of love: *"Let all your things be done with charity (love)"* (1 Corinthians 16:14). All of us are guilty of poor judgment and committing sins, but our service to the Lord can still be beneficial when we are serving in the power of love. *"And above all things have fervent charity among yourselves: for charity shall cover the multitude of sins"* (1 Peter 4:8). Love for God and love for people are excellent reasons to do our best in Christian service, and we can be certain that good things will come as a result.

The Apostle Paul was evidently a very intelligent, educated and talented man, but he didn't depend on any of his personal abilities when he attempted to do something for the Lord. He made it very clear that all that he did was because of the grace of God working through him. *"But by the grace of God I am what I am: and his grace which was bestowed upon me was not in vain; but I laboured more abundantly than they all: yet not I, but the grace of God which was with me"* (1 Corinthians 15:10). No matter how talented our bodies may be, the world does not need what we can do through natural abilities, but what the grace of God can do through us. Before attempting anything for the Lord, we need to pray for His grace to flow through us as we serve: *"Wherefore we receiving a kingdom which cannot be moved, let us have grace, whereby we may serve God acceptably with reverence and godly fear"* (Hebrews 12:28). It is God's grace that makes our labors acceptable to God and to others.

Submitting to the Lordship of Jesus, living in obedience to the Word of God, being motivated by love, and depending on the power of God's grace are each very important because they are things that the Holy Spirit will use to do His work in our lives. It is only when we are committed to allowing the Spirit to use us that we can be certain that our labor will not be in vain. *"Therefore, my beloved brethren, be ye stedfast, unmoveable, always abounding in the work of the Lord, forasmuch as ye know that your labour is not in vain in the Lord"* (1 Corinthians 15:58). It is through the Holy Spirit that we are able to grow from babes in Christ to strong productive Christians. *"But grow in grace, and in the knowledge of our Lord and Saviour Jesus Christ. To him be glory both now and for ever. Amen"* (2 Peter 3:18). As this growth commences, more and more Christian characteristics will be found in us that will make our fruitfulness a certainty.

> *"And beside this, giving all diligence, add to your faith virtue; and to virtue knowledge; And to knowledge temperance; and to temperance patience; and to patience godliness; And to godliness brotherly kindness; and to brotherly kindness charity. For if these things be in you, and abound, they make you that ye shall neither be barren nor unfruitful in the knowledge of our Lord Jesus Christ"* (2 Peter 1:5-8)

The primary purpose of every Christian should be to bring glory to God: *"Whether therefore ye eat, or drink, or whatsoever ye do, do all to the glory of God"* (1 Corinthians 10:31). As we are involved in bringing glory to God, we will also bring many blessings to the people who dwell around us. Being committed to the glory of God and to the good of people will also bring something to us – greater rewards in Heaven! It will also give us the joy and satisfaction of knowing that we are being the people of God who are doing the work of God in a way that is pleasing to Him.

The spiritual principles presented above can be used in every Christian life to insure that commitment to God will bring about wonderful blessings with assured certainty. There are also scientific principles whereby scientists can be committed to using God's physical laws with certainty about what the result will be. It is quite ironic that a scientist who claims to be an atheist still commits himself to use the physical laws of God with confidence.

The chemist can combine two parts of hydrogen, one part of sulfur, and four parts of oxygen (H_2SO_4) with all confidence that the solution will become sulfuric acid. The space scientist uses the physical laws of motion to design trajectories and orbital maneuvers for his desired missions. If he is correct in his engineering and equations, he can be confident that whatever he commits to the laws of physics will bring about the certain results that he desires.

From 1962 – 72, I worked as an aerospace engineer in our nation's space program. I began at the George C. Marshall Space Flight Center in Huntsville, Alabama. My job responsibilities involved designing trajectories that would place satellites in desired orbits. Following the flight, the actual trajectory would be determined from tracking data. The actual trajectory would be compared to the predicted to ascertain any differences, and then the reason for variances had to be determined.

When our nation instituted the program to go to the moon, a new NASA facility was built near Houston, Texas, that was named the Manned Spacecraft Center. It has been re-named the Johnson Space Center. This venture fascinated me so I asked for and was granted a transfer to Houston in March, 1964. I was assigned to the Theoretical Mechanics Branch of the Guidance and Control Division. It was our responsibility to develop and check out guidance equations for space flights that would take place several years in the future. Each engineer had his own area of assignment for the various parts of the space mission. I was responsible for the descent and ascent equations that would guide the vehicle from its orbit around the moon to the lunar landing, and then get it back safely into orbit. The final decision on which set of equations would be used was made in 1965, and they were used for the first time by astronauts Neil Armstrong and Buzz Aldrin in 1969.

The manufacturing and engineering associated with the Saturn 1-B and Saturn V programs were moved from Huntsville, Alabama, to the Michoud Operations Facility in New Orleans, Louisiana, while I was in Houston. Since my wife and I had both grown up in south Mississippi and New Orleans was near to both of our families, I left Houston to work at Michoud in March, 1966. I was assigned to the same responsibilities that I had in Huntsville in designing trajectories and then using tracking data to calculate the actual flight. Later, I became the supervisor of the Orbital Determination Unit and our group had the responsibility of taking tracking data from radar stations around the earth to determine the actual orbit of a satellite.

I left my work in the space industry to answer God's call to the ministry in February, 1972. I am sure that the methods that we used during those early years of space exploration are very primitive compared to what modern engineers are doing today. Much of our work was done with paper and pencil. Most engineers had the use of electric adding machines that would only do the mathematical functions of adding, subtracting, multiplying and dividing. We used graph paper to plot our data by hand. We had to use a book of tables to find our trigonometric and logarithmic constants. At Marshall and Michoud there were computer centers where a programmer was assigned to work with certain engineers, but no engineer had the use of a personal computer.

While at the Manned Spacecraft Center, I did my own programming since the Guidance and Control Division had its own computer department. The computer was an IBM 7094 that had 32,000 bits of location, yet it filled a very large room. Today, you can hold a computer in your hand that contains several million bits of location and is probably a thousand times faster!

I feel very blessed to have had the opportunity to be involved in the early days of our space industry even though we were on the very cutting edge. There is no doubt that I would be totally lost if I had to enter those work forces again since things have changed so much. Many things that we were doing for the first time have now been done repeatedly and the years of experience have fine tuned the processes and improved the results.

There are some things, however, that have not changed through all of these years – the physical laws of God that control our universe! The most modern engineer may have the latest machines and methods, but he is still restrained by the constraints placed on him by the very laws that God used in creating all things. It is only when an engineer is committed to using and obeying those physical laws that he can be certain of the success of his mission.

Since I am not involved with modern space exploration and the work of those who are currently working in that industry, I am not familiar with the latest guidance techniques for powered flight or orbital maneuvers. They are surely much more efficient than what was used when I was involved, but the methods that we used would still work today since the laws of motion have not changed.

I believe that God gave me the experience of working in the space industry prior to calling me into the ministry so that I would have the following information to share with others. God is faithful! When we are committed to obeying His laws, whether they are physical or spiritual, it is certain what the outcome will be!

Predicted Trajectory

Before an engineer can design a trajectory, there are some very important and pertinent information that he must be given. Someone has to decide exactly what orbit is desired. What will be the altitude of the orbit and the azimuth of the flight? The azimuth is the angle measured from north to the direction of the flight (see Figure 8-4). The shape of the vehicle has to be supplied to determine the effects of drag as it is going through the atmosphere. Information such as the expected lift off weight, combined thrusts of the engines, flow rate of fuel, etc., is necessary to calculate the acceleration throughout the powered flight. Integral calculus uses the acceleration to determine the velocity, location and direction of travel at any time.

Typically, the vehicle will be placed on the launch pad with Fin 1 pointing in the eastern direction (see Figure 8-1). If the desired azimuth is 80°, the vehicle will go into a roll program as soon as it clears the launch pad so that the ZB axis of the body fixed coordinate system is pointing down range. Thus, the XB – ZB plane of the body fixed coordinate system will be aligned with the XL – ZL plane from the earth fixed coordinate system (Figure 8-2). At approximately 10 seconds, the vehicle will begin its pitch maneuver to start its flight down range.

Information given in the previous chapter revealed that a circular orbit of 100 nautical miles requires a horizontal velocity of 25,573.4 ft/sec. A pitch program has to be determined, therefore, that will guide the vehicle so that it will merge into that altitude at exactly that velocity. Obviously, the vehicle cannot go straight up until it is 100 miles high and then make a right hand turn! If it starts pitching over too fast, it may be half way around the earth before it ever reaches the desired altitude. There is an optimum trajectory that will guide the vehicle to the desired altitude and velocity with the direction of motion lying in the horizontal plane (perpendicular to the radius from the center of gravity of the earth) in the shortest amount of time.

Since the flow rate of the fuel is relatively constant, a shorter time of flight means that less fuel is required. With less fuel being required, the size of the payload of the satellite that can be inserted into orbit will be maximized.

Once the optimum roll and pitch programs are determined, the predicted trajectory can be calculated with the expected location and velocity being presented in the earth fixed, inertial, and earth centered coordinate systems throughout the flight. For example, the engineer can look at the trajectory data at 100 seconds after liftoff and know the expected location, altitude, velocity, direction of travel, etc., at that point in the flight.

It is important that the reader have an appreciation for the precision that is needed to place a satellite in orbit. Now, to believe that the moon was placed in orbit around the earth and all the planets around the sun by an accident is foolishness! No mathematical model can be found that will duplicate an accident that would produce the solar system, including all the moons orbiting their respective planets! Especially, when considering that some of the moons are going in opposite directions around the same planet. It was all by an act of God and all He had to do was say, "Let it be!"

Actual Flight

The roll and pitch programs determined in the predicted trajectory are provided to the mission control engineers who prepare the vehicle for flight. All the pertinent information is programmed into the onboard computer to guide the vehicle on its mission. Throughout the flight, the computer is constantly comparing its actual location, speed and direction to that which was prescribed.

The acceleration in the predicted trajectory was calculated (Equation 8-3) using the expected force and mass of the vehicle, but in the actual flight the acceleration is not calculated – it is measured! There are three accelerometers aligned with the XB, YB, and ZB axes of the body fixed coordinate system. These accelerometers sense the acceleration in each of these directions as soon as the vehicle lifts off the launch pad. The computer continues to receive the measurements throughout the flight and uses integral calculus to determine the location, velocity, and direction (including the pitch, yaw, and roll angles) at any time in flight.

Since these accelerometers are aligned with the three axes, they are each at 90^0 angles to each other. This creates a three dimensional system where any movement is actually known. Once again, we are obligated to God for teaching us! Have you ever considered how you know whether you are standing or lying down by your senses? When you close your eyes, you can still sense whether your head is moving or not. How? God has built into each ear three semicircular canals that work in a similar way as accelerometers! They sense any movement of the head and transmit the information to the brain.

> The inner ear (labyrinth) is a complete structure consisting of two major parts: the cochlea, the organ of hearing, and the vestibular system, the organ of balance. The vestibular system consists of the saccule and the utricle, which determine position sense, and the semicircular canals, which help maintain balance.

> The semicircular canals are three fluid-filled tubes at right angles to one another. Movement of the head causes the fluid in the canals to move. Depending on the direction the head moves, the fluid movement will be greater in one of the canals than in the others. The

canals contain hair cells that respond to this movement of fluid. The hair cells initiate nerve impulses that tell the brain which way the head is moving, so that appropriate action can be taken to maintain balance.

If the semicircular canals malfunction, as may occur in an upper respiratory infection and other conditions both temporary and permanent, a person's sense of balance may be lost or a whirling sensation (vertigo) may develop.[75]

All that the engineer does in installing accelerometers is copying what God did when He designed the ear! Yet, there are people who try to teach that everything about us and all of the animal kingdom is because of evolution. How foolish!

The onboard computer guides the vehicle into the horizontal plane at the appropriate altitude while also maintaining its location and movement in the orbital plane at the desired azimuth. The computer keeps the vehicle in the horizontal plane (the same altitude above the earth) until the required velocity is reached and then commands the engines to shut off. The vehicle is now in orbit where God's physical laws will keep it.

Sometimes super glue is used to connect items together. After an appropriate time for drying, they will be gently released to see if the gluing was successful. A large picture may be hung on the wall and be held partially in place by the installer's hands to make certain that the hanger is strong enough to hold it. But when a space vehicle is inserted into orbit, the astronaut does not have to hold his breath to see whether or not it is going to stay. If the requirements for an orbit are reached, the vehicle will remain in orbit until some other force acts on it to change its speed or direction of motion. When you commit to God's requirements, the outcome is certain!

Observed Trajectory

There are tracking sites located in the area of the launch and flight path so that the vehicle will be observed by radar from the time of its lift off throughout its powered flight. The radar measures the distance of the vehicle from the particular radar site, its elevation above the horizontal plane, and the angle of the vehicle relative to the direction of north. Using these parameters, the location of the vehicle can be calculated relative to the launch pad as (XL, YL, ZL) of the earth fixed coordinate system (Figure 8-2). Thus, the displacement (or location) of the vehicle is known by observation during the entire time of its powered trajectory.

In the predicted trajectory the acceleration was calculated using the expected thrust and mass of the vehicle while the onboard accelerometers measure the acceleration in the actual flight. In each case, integral calculus was used to determine the velocity and displacement at any time in the flight. The first integral of acceleration gives the velocity while the second integral provides the current location. The reverse of this procedure is used in the observed trajectory.

The observed (XL, YL, ZL) displacement can be used to determine the velocity and acceleration along each of the three axes. Differential calculus is used to perform this task. The first derivative of displacement gives the velocity and the second determines the acceleration. Thus, observing the continual location enables one to also calculate the velocity and acceleration along the respective axes.

<u>Orbital Maneuvers</u>

Once a satellite is safely in its orbit, there are numerous other maneuvers that can be accomplished. Thus far, only the parameters of a circular orbit have been presented where the vehicle remains the same distance above the earth. There are times, however, when an elliptical orbit is required where the altitude above the earth varies from its perigee (the lowest point) to the apogee (the highest point). The maneuver of going from a circular to an elliptical orbit is easily accomplished. The velocity the satellite is traveling is always the highest at its perigee. After it passes though its perigee, it continues to slow down until it reaches the apogee at which time it begins to accelerate again.

A German scientist, Walter Hohmann, published a paper in 1925 where he described how a spacecraft in one circular orbit can be moved to another using two firings of the engines. The procedure has been appropriately called the "Hohmann Transfer." You will notice that his writing took place over 30 years prior to America launching her first satellite!

For our example, we will consider moving the satellite from a circular orbit of 100 nautical miles to one of 200 nautical miles. The Hohmann Transfer involves calculating the velocity that will be required at perigee and apogee for an elliptical orbit that is 100 X 200 nautical miles. With the vehicle in its circular orbit, the engines will fire keeping the vehicle's motion in the horizontal and orbital planes while increasing the velocity to that which the perigee requires. At that point, the engines are shut off and the vehicle is at the perigee in the desired elliptical orbit. If the burn was accurately performed, there is absolute confidence that after 180° the vehicle will be at an altitude of 200 nautical miles! The engines would fire once again to increase the speed to circularize the orbit at that altitude.

A similar maneuver is required when one vehicle is trying to rendezvous with another in space. I was working at the Manned Spacecraft Center in Houston when Col. James McDivitt attempted America's first rendezvous. His effort to perform the procedure failed. We had an analog simulator (which was like their space capsule) in our building where the astronauts could come and practice their various maneuvers. We were told that he had not used it because he was an excellent pilot and didn't think he needed to practice. Mr. Jack Funk was my supervisor as the head of the Theoretical Mechanics Branch and I have always remembered his response, "For a pilot to think he can get in a spacecraft and fly it the same way he does a plane is as foolish as a farmer getting in a jet and saying 'giddy up'!" His comment received a lot of laughs, but it was also very true.

For the sake of simplicity, we will consider two spacecrafts in the same orbit but one is 15 minutes behind the other one. For the one in front to attempt a maneuver with the one trailing it, you might think the one in front would need to slow down. But if it slowed down it would leave a circular orbit and its altitude would become the apogee of an elliptical orbit, which would have a faster period for one revolution. Rather than getting closer to the other spacecraft, it would in fact begin getting farther away. But if the astronaut in front increases his speed, he is making his altitude the perigee of an elliptical orbit. Therefore, he can change his circular orbit to an elliptical orbit that increases the orbital period by 15 minutes. After one orbit he would return to the perigee (which is the same altitude as the other spacecraft) and they would be together! He would then slow his vehicle down so it would be back in a circular orbit. In like manner, the orbital period can be increased by 3 minutes and they will be near to each other in 5 orbits.

If the spacecraft that is behind attempts to catch up with the one in front, he must slow down! This would place him in an elliptical orbit with a shorter orbital period so that each orbit would bring them closer together. Once the space-crafts are near to each other, the one that has been making the maneuvers will adjust his speed to return to the same orbit as the other spacecraft. Final small maneuvers can be made to join the spacecrafts together.

This is an interesting but true concept of a rendezvous in orbital flight. To catch up with someone in front of you, you must slow down. To allow someone behind you to catch up, you must speed up. In each case, the astronaut can make the maneuvers with confidence. If his calculations are correct and he applies the engine thrusts properly, he can rest with certainty that he has committed his spacecraft to the desired end!

Trans-Lunar Injection

One of the most intriguing orbital maneuvers occurs when a spacecraft in orbit around the earth fires its engines to be inserted on a path to the moon! A maneuver very similar to the Hohmann Transfer can be used to calculate the velocity that is needed to escape the earth orbit and cause the spacecraft to pass near the moon's surface. Typically, the length of the flight is determined and the engines are fired 180° on the opposite side of the earth from where the moon will be in its orbit at the time the spacecraft arrives. For our purposes, we will assume that the plan is to insert the spacecraft in a circular orbit that is 50,000 feet above the lunar surface.

As the spacecraft leaves the earth's orbit, it will begin slowing down just as if it was in an elliptical orbit moving from perigee towards apogee. But, now there will be two gravitational forces acting on it! As it moves away from earth, the gravitational pull of the earth will begin to diminish as the pull from the moon's gravity is increasing. The vehicle will continue to slow down until the pull from the moon becomes greater than that from earth. At this time, the vehicle will begin accelerating again.

It is very important that the vehicle continue using its location and movement to project ahead what its location will be when it nears the moon. Remember, the moon is moving also and the astronaut surely doesn't want to fly straight into it! To be sure that he will be passing the moon at an altitude of 50,000 feet, the astronaut will make some 'mid-course corrections' to insure that he is on the right path. That is much like the life of a Christian.

It is also important for every Christian to examine the direction of his life from time to time. If we are honest with ourselves, most of us will admit that our lives and service to the Lord are not really what we want them to be! Each of us have planned on what we want to be doing for the Lord some day, but we never seem to reach that 'some day'. That is why it is important for every Christian to make 'mid-course corrections'!

We know where we are and the direction we are currently going. We need to make changes to be sure we become what we want, and to have a safe arrival at our desired position. That was the attitude of the Apostle Paul when he penned the following words.

> *"Not as though I had already attained, either were already perfect: but I follow after, if that I may apprehend that for which also I am apprehended of Christ Jesus. Brethren, I count not myself to have apprehended: but this one thing I do, forgetting those things which are behind, and reaching forth unto those things which are before, I press toward the mark for the prize of the high calling of God in Christ Jesus"* (Philippians 3:12-14)

Each Christian needs to constantly make rededications and commitments in an effort to have a closer walk with the Lord!

As the spacecraft passes the moon at 50,000 feet, it will be traveling at a speed that could cause it to 'whip' around the moon and head on into space or back toward earth in an elliptical orbit. But, as it is passing the moon at the desired altitude, the astronaut will reverse the spacecraft and fire the engines to slow it down to the required velocity for a circular orbit. It will then be in its lunar orbit. A similar maneuver will be used for its trans-earth injection when it is time to come home.

꩜

Some principles of powered flight and orbital maneuvers have been presented to reveal the simplicity (and yet complexity) that is required in the exploration of space. Hopefully, the reader will have an appreciation for the precision that is required for successful missions. More importantly, each reader should have a fresh appreciation for all that God did in creating all things. The space scientist is limited to using the physical laws that God has established in performing his tasks.

Knowing what is required for a man-made satellite to be placed in orbit around the earth should cause anyone to reject the theory that the moon was placed in its orbit by accident! Even when a person does not accept the Biblical account of creation, the laws of physics should cause anyone to reject an accidental orbit from an arbitrary event.

Some have theorized that the earth was a spinning mass when it contracted into a globe and the moon was 'cast off' into its orbit where it also contracted into a globe. Had this happened, the moon would likely have gone off in a tangential direction and not into an orbit!

Others have presented the theory that the moon came from some other place and as it traveled though space it happened to pass 240,000 miles from the earth and was 'captured' in its orbit by the gravitational force of the earth. It is total foolishness to even consider the possibility that the moon just happened to go past the earth at the right altitude and velocity to place it suddenly in an orbit. It is absolutely amazing to see what some people will believe while refusing to accept the truth that all things were designed and created by the power of God!

The possibility of an accident bringing the solar system into existence is further compounded when considering all the planets in orbit around the sun and the many moons which are in orbit around their respective planets. There is the distinct possibility that the entire solar system is also in orbit around some other force. Simply put, only God could have done it all!

It is incumbent on each of us to learn all the laws of God and be committed to obeying them. The spiritual laws He has established will direct us in the service we give Him. As we obey those laws, He will be glorified, others will be blessed, and we will be rewarded in Heaven! It is absolutely certain!

The physical laws that we live under were designed and provided for our benefit. As we live under the influence of those laws, God should be thanked, others will benefit, and we will be reminded of the faithfulness of God. These are laws of science that can be committed to with certainty! There are other sciences that are not so trustworthy.

There are so many areas of our lives that are controlled by the various social sciences (such as psychology and sociology) that are not so dependable. A defendant may be on trial for some horrible crime and the prosecuting attorney and defense attorney will each present a Psychologist to give testimony about him. The Psychologists may be equally qualified, yet their analysis and testimony may be exactly opposite.

Several Sociologists can be hired to study what can be done to revitalize a portion of a city and improve the lives of the citizens. Yet, their opinions and recommendations may be totally different. Not one of them can guarantee that his recommendations will work and have any lasting results. It is not an exact science!

These social sciences depend somewhat on man and his own reasoning ability. The physical sciences depend on God! He has established them and, therefore, they can not be changed. It is the wise person who sees God and learns to use the physical laws He has established. It is also the wise person who sees the physical laws that control the universe and recognizes there had to be a God Who instituted them. A commitment to Him is a commitment to all His laws and His response makes the outcome certain. *"Commit thy way unto the LORD; trust also in him; and he shall bring it to pass"* (Psalm 37:5).

Chapter 10
SALVATION PRESENTED IN CREATION'S STORY

The Bible is the most unique book ever written by man! While it was written by the hands of men, it is in fact the Word of God and presents the thoughts from the very heart of God. There were approximately forty men who were used as writers of the various books of the Bible but none of them took credit for the words that they wrote. It is emphasized repeatedly that it was the Holy Spirit who inspired each and every word in the original writings.

"All scripture is given by inspiration of God, and is profitable for doctrine, for reproof, for correction, for instruction in righteousness" (2 Timothy 3:16)

"Now we have received, not the spirit of the world, but the spirit which is of God; that we might know the things that are freely given to us of God. Which things also we speak, not in the words which man's wisdom teacheth, but which the Holy Ghost teacheth; comparing spiritual things with spiritual" (1 Corinthians 2:12, 13)

"For the prophecy came not in old time by the will of man: but holy men of God spake as they were moved by the Holy Ghost" (2 Peter 1:21)

The Apostle Peter stated that the commandments of the Apostles in the New Testament were to be accepted on an equal basis with the words of the prophets that are found in the Old Testament.

"This second epistle, beloved, I now write unto you; in both which I stir up your pure minds by way of remembrance: That ye may be mindful of the words which were spoken before by the holy prophets, and of the commandment of us the apostles of the Lord and Saviour" (2 Peter 3:1, 2)

It should be obvious that God had very special plans for how His Word would be used for Him to be so meticulous in providing it for us.

The Bible begins in the first chapter declaring that God is the Creator of all things. In particular, He created the first man, Adam, in His own image as someone who would be able to have fellowship with his Creator. In the third chapter, however, Eve ate of the forbidden fruit and Adam followed her in the transgression, breaking the sweet fellowship they enjoyed with God. The rest of the Bible details the efforts of God to reconcile fallen man to Himself whereby they could once again enjoy a fellowship of righteousness.

The commandments that He gave are not only for His glory, but also for the benefit of each individual who obeys them and for the betterment of all society. He never gave a "Thou shalt not" against anything that would be good for us!

In like manner, each time He said "Thou shalt" it was always for things that are good and holy. Everyone benefits when God's Word is obeyed, yet it is primarily God's revelation to each individual where His will and ways are made known so that all will know how to please God.

There are many scientific truths in the Bible, but it is not a science book. There are many historical facts presented about nations and individuals of which we would never be aware except for the details given in the Bible. Yet, it is not a history book! Instructions and warnings are given concerning health for our bodies, but it is not a medical journal. It is given to remind each individual of his personal accountability and responsibility before a holy God! It presents God's plan of salvation to fallen man and reveals God's will for all who accept His great salvation!

It is God's will that each one who is saved will grow into a mature and productive Christian. *"But grow in grace, and in the knowledge of our Lord and Saviour Jesus Christ. To him be glory both now and for ever. Amen"* (2 Peter 3:18). The Word of God is as necessary for that growth as milk is for a newborn infant. *"As newborn babes, desire the sincere milk of the word, that ye may grow thereby"* (1 Peter 2:2). Without this growth, the new Christian will remain a babe in Christ and live a carnal rather than spiritual life.

> *"And I, brethren, could not speak unto you as unto spiritual, but as unto carnal, even as unto babes in Christ. I have fed you with milk, and not with meat: for hitherto ye were not able to bear it, neither yet now are ye able. For ye are yet carnal: for whereas there is among you envying,*

and strife, and divisions, are ye not carnal, and walk as men?" (1 Corinthians 3:1-3)

A steady diet on the Word of God is absolutely necessary for the young Christian to grow. It is equally essential for the mature Christian to continue to feed on the Word to retain spiritual strength and vitality! Unlike physical growth, a Christian's spiritual growth never ceases when given a steady diet of God's Word.

Since every Christian lives in the midst of a sinful world, it is imperative that he is careful to not become like the world. It is the Bible that directs the path and keeps one from evil: *"Thy word is a lamp unto my feet, and a light unto my path"* (Psalm 119:105) and *"Thy word have I hid in mine heart, that I might not sin against thee"* (Psalm 119:11). Unfortunately, people do stray into sin because they do not always obey the Scriptures, and yet the Word is still available to cleanse them. *"Where-withal shall a young man cleanse his way? by taking heed thereto according to thy word"* (Psalm 119:9). Therefore, it is the Word of God that helps to keep us in fellowship with God, but it is also used to restore that fellowship when it is broken.

God did not just save us to keep us from hell and give us a home in heaven, but also that we may be His servants while we live here on earth. After assuring us that all Scripture was inspired of God in 2 Timothy 3:16 (as given above), the next verse reveals the affects it will have on the man of God: *"That the man of God may be perfect* (or mature), *thoroughly furnished unto all good works"* (2 Timothy 3:17) (Emphasis mine). In the previous chapter, Paul had stated that one who studies the Word will be a 'workman': *"Study to show thyself approved unto*

God, a workman that needeth not to be ashamed, rightly dividing the word of truth" (2 Timothy 2:15). It should be evident that the Word of God is absolutely essential for us to become the servants of God who are pleasing to Him.

Meditation on the Word of God will cause us to have the proper affect on those who live around us and guarantee the efficiency of our own fruitfulness in our service for the Lord. Surely, the one who meditates on the Word of God is a blessed man!

> *"Blessed is the man that walketh not in the counsel of the ungodly, nor standeth in the way of sinners, nor sitteth in the seat of the scornful. But his delight is in the law of the LORD; and in his law doth he meditate day and night. And he shall be like a tree planted by the rivers of water, that bringeth forth his fruit in his season; his leaf also shall not wither; and whatsoever he doeth shall prosper"* (Psalms 1:1-3)

While the Scriptures are so important in the life of the Christian, they are even more beneficial as they present the plan of salvation whereby a sinner can know how to become a child of God. The Apostle Paul reminded Timothy that the Scriptures were used to lead him to salvation: *"And that from a child thou hast known the holy scriptures, which are able to make thee wise unto salvation through faith which is in Christ Jesus"* (2 Timothy 3:15). Thankfully, the gospel that was used to win Timothy to salvation is equally effective for everyone else who will believe in Jesus Christ. *"For I am not ashamed of the gospel of Christ: for it is the power of God unto salvation to every one that believeth; to the Jew first, and also to the Greek"* (Romans 1:16).

There are many texts found in the Bible that present the plan of salvation in very simple terms. Possibly, no text has been used more effectively than some of the verses that are found in Chapter 10 of Romans. The chapter opens with Paul recognizing the zeal of the Jews as they tried to gain righteousness through their own works because they did not have proper knowledge of God's righteousness. He then presented that salvation is only available through faith in Jesus Christ, and that faith is based on the truth of the gospel presented in the Bible.

> *"That if thou shalt confess with thy mouth the Lord Jesus, and shalt believe in thine heart that God hath raised him from the dead, thou shalt be saved. For with the heart man believeth unto righteousness; and with the mouth confession is made unto salvation — For whosoever shall call upon the name of the Lord shall be saved. How then shall they call on him in whom they have not believed? and how shall they believe in him of whom they have not heard? and how shall they hear without a preacher? — So then faith cometh by hearing, and hearing by the word of God"* (Romans 10:9, 10, 13, 14, 17).

Salvation is not only presented in texts such as these, but many historical events found in the Bible also present a picture of the gospel message and the salvation of a soul who trusts Jesus Christ.

A picture of the gospel message was presented immediately after the sin of Adam and Eve when God provided a covering for their nakedness. *"Unto Adam also and to his wife did the LORD God make coats of skins, and clothed them"* (Genesis 3:21). It is evident that an innocent animal had to die for skins to be available. Thus, the principle of the innocent dying for the guilty began as a prophetic message of the gospel - about how Jesus would one day die for all guilty sinners.

It was in the Garden of Eden that God instituted the entire sacrificial system which was symbolic of the coming death of Jesus on Calvary's cross, and the principle that sins could only be forgiven by the offering of a blood sacrifice. Abel followed the example when *"he also brought of the firstlings of his flock and of the fat thereof"* (Genesis 4:4). When Noah took animals two by two into the ark to preserve life after the flood, he also took clean animals to offer as sacrifices to God after the flood had ended.

> *"And Noah builded an altar unto the LORD; and took of every clean beast, and of every clean fowl, and offered burnt offerings on the altar. And the LORD smelled a sweet savour; and the LORD said in his heart, I will not again curse the ground any more for man's sake; for the imagination of man's heart is evil from his youth; neither will I again smite any more every thing living, as I have done"* (Genesis 8:20, 21)

All the sacrifices in the Old Testament involved the offering of blood from an innocent animal for the forgiveness of the guilty sinner. The gospel of Jesus was being proclaimed each time an animal died!

When Abraham took Isaac up on Mt. Moriah to offer him as a sacrifice, it was a picture of how God, the Father, would one day offer His Son, Jesus Christ.

"And he said, Take now thy son, thine only son Isaac, whom thou lovest, and get thee into the land of Moriah; and offer him there for a burnt offering upon one of the mountains which I will tell thee of. And Abraham rose up early in the morning, and saddled his ass, and took two of his young men with him, and Isaac his son, and clave the wood for the burnt offering, and rose up, and went unto the place of which God had told him. Then on the third day Abraham lifted up his eyes, and saw the place afar off" (Genesis 22:2-4)

Isaac was as good as dead in the heart of Abraham on the three day journey to Mt. Moriah. When God provided the ram as a substitute, Isaac was resurrected in the heart of his father.

"By faith Abraham, when he was tried, offered up Isaac: and he that had received the promises offered up his only begotten son, Of whom it was said, That in Isaac shall thy seed be called: Accounting that God was able to raise him up, even from the dead; from whence also he received him in a figure" (Hebrews 11:17-19)

In this account, Jesus was not only pictured by Isaac, but also by the ram that died as a substitute so that Isaac could live. While events such as this present the gospel message, there are others that picture what happens to a soul when it is saved from sin.

A flood was used to destroy the wicked generation that lived on earth in Noah's day. The ark that he prepared is a beautiful type of Jesus Christ. It was made according to the instructions given by God to save people from a coming judgment. Once it was ready, God invited the people to come in: *"And the LORD said unto Noah, Come thou and all thy house into the ark"* (Genesis 7:1). Those who entered were totally secure from the judgment that fell on those who were outside of the ark of safety. *"And they that went in, went in male and female of all flesh, as God had commanded him: and the LORD shut him in"* (Genesis 7:16). The New Testament compares the physical salvation of the souls in the ark to those who are spiritually saved by Jesus Christ.

> *"Which sometime were disobedient, when once the long-suffering of God waited in the days of Noah, while the ark was a preparing, wherein few, that is, eight souls were saved by water. The like figure whereunto even baptism doth also now save us (not the putting away of the filth of the flesh, but the answer of a good conscience toward God,) by the resurrection of Jesus Christ: Who is gone into heaven, and is on the right hand of God; angels and authorities and powers being made subject unto him"* (1 Peter 3:20-22)

It is evident that the eight souls were saved by the ark and not the water. It was the water that separated them from the ungodly. In like manner, Christian baptism does not save the soul, but is an act of obedience whereby the believer separates himself from the unbelieving world. Therefore, this act of obedience is "the answer of a good conscience toward God."

The exodus of Israel from the bondage they suffered in the land of Egypt is another picture of salvation. Their bondage in Egypt is a picture of the spiritual bondage of a sinner who is limited in what he can do and is suffering under the tremendous weight of his sins. The physical salvation of the Jews was a blood bought redemption as an innocent lamb had to die for the death angel to pass over them. In like manner, Jesus is the Passover Lamb for each sinner: *"For even Christ our passover is sacrificed for us"* (1 Corinthians 5:7). As they passed through the Red Sea, they symbolized our baptism as we go forth to serve God after being saved: *"And were all baptized unto Moses in the cloud and in the sea"* (1 Corinthians 10:2).

Moses reminded the people that salvation was only available through the power of God. They had to cease all personal efforts for salvation and simply trust God to receive what only He was able to do!

"And Moses said unto the people, Fear ye not, stand still, and see the salvation of the LORD, which he will show to you to day: for the Egyptians whom ye have seen to day, ye shall see them again no more for ever. The LORD shall fight for you, and ye shall hold your peace" (Exodus 14:13, 14)

Their salvation depended on the supernatural power of God. So does ours!

The best known verse in all the Bible is John 3:16 and it very simply (yet very profoundly) presents the salvation that is available in Jesus Christ. Yet many are not aware of the Old Testament event that led to this verse being found in the New Testament.

The children of Israel were on their journey through the wilderness when they began to complain against God and Moses about the difficulties they faced. Rather than providing their needs, God sent fiery serpents to bite them resulting in many deaths.

> *"And the people spake against God, and against Moses, Wherefore have ye brought us up out of Egypt to die in the wilderness? for there is no bread, neither is there any water; and our soul loatheth this light bread. And the LORD sent fiery serpents among the people, and they bit the people; and much people of Israel died"* (Numbers 21:5, 6)

This judgment caused the people to come to Moses confessing their sins and asking for God's deliverance.

> *"Therefore the people came to Moses, and said, We have sinned, for we have spoken against the LORD, and against thee; pray unto the LORD, that he take away the serpents from us. And Moses prayed for the people. And the LORD said unto Moses, Make thee a fiery serpent, and set it upon a pole: and it shall come to pass, that every one that is bitten, when he looketh upon it, shall live. And Moses made a serpent of brass, and put it upon a pole, and it came to pass, that if a serpent had bitten any man, when he beheld the serpent of brass, he lived"* (Numbers 21:7-9)

This is an event that should be a warning to everyone who would dare to complain against God and those He has placed over them! It is a message of judgment, but also a beautiful picture of the salvation that is available through Jesus Christ!

It was over 1500 years after the event of the fiery serpents that a man named Nicodemus came to Jesus by night. As a Pharisee and a ruler of the Jews, Nicodemus knew the Bible very well and was acquainted with all the historical things that had happened to the Jews. Yet, he was astonished when Jesus told him that he had to be born again before he would ever see the kingdom of God. *"Jesus answered and said unto him, Verily, verily, I say unto thee, Except a man be born again, he cannot see the kingdom of God"* (John 3:3). As Jesus explained what it was to be born again, He took an event that Nicodemus was familiar with to present the message of the gospel.

> *"And as Moses lifted up the serpent in the wilderness, even so must the Son of man be lifted up: That whosoever believeth in him should not perish, but have eternal life. For God so loved the world, that he gave his only begotten Son, that whosoever believeth in him should not perish, but have everlasting life"* (John 3:14-16)

When God sent the judgment on the complaining Jews, He was really presenting a picture of the salvation that would one day be provided through Jesus Christ!

The serpent that bit them could be symbolic of the devil who has bitten every person. Also, it was a serpent that brought death, but another serpent was used to restore life. In like manner, it was the first man Adam that brought death and it took another man Jesus to overcome the curse. *"Forasmuch then as the children are partakers of flesh and blood, he also himself likewise took part of the same; that through death he might destroy him that had the power of death, that is, the devil"* (Hebrews 2:14). The offer of salvation was universal – every one who was bitten could look and live! But, there is something else about a serpent on a pole that presents our Savior.

When Jesus said *"As Moses lifted up the serpent in the wilderness, even so must the Son of man be lifted up"*, you know Jesus was referring to His cross. The serpent was lifted up on a pole so that it was in sight of anyone who was bitten and every 'whosoever' could immediately look and live. Jesus invites all to look to Him and live. *"Look unto me, and be ye saved, all the ends of the earth: for I am God, and there is none else"* (Isaiah 45:22). It is from His lifted up position on the cross that He invites all sinners to come: *"And I, if I be lifted up from the earth, will draw all men unto me. This he said, signifying what death he should die"* (John 12:32, 33).

We should not be surprised to find simple events from the Old Testament being used to present the beautiful story of salvation. The Bible is not history, but 'His-story'. It is all about Jesus and what He can do for fallen man. The real message of the Bible is salvation for fallen man.

The details about the creation of the earth and the creation of Adam are two of the most outstanding events presented in our Bible. I believe that God's creation story of the earth also presents His salvation story for man. What has already happened to the earth and what has been promised to occur in the future presents a parallel to what happens in the life of one who has been saved by the grace of God. If simple occurrences in the Old Testament were used to present the gospel and examples of salvation, we should expect that something as great as the creation and history of planet earth would do the same. Read on to see that indeed this is the case!

The Original Earth

The creation of the earth is presented in the first verse found in the Bible. *"In the beginning God created the heaven and the earth"* (Genesis 1:1). This act of God (like all of His work) was done to perfection. This original earth was very beautiful because the angels began to rejoice and shout for joy when they observed it for the first time. *"Where wast thou when I laid the foundations of the earth? — When the morning stars sang together, and all the sons of God shouted for joy?"* (Job 38:4a, 7). The same angels who rejoiced at seeing the newly created earth also see the birth of every little baby that is born.

That night in Bethlehem when the virgin Mary gave birth to baby Jesus the angels rejoiced and immediately went to shepherds to announce the wonderful news of His birth.

> *"And there were in the same country shepherds abiding in the field, keeping watch over their flock by night. And, lo, the angel of the Lord came upon them, and the glory of the Lord shone round about them: and they were sore afraid. And the angel said unto them, Fear not: for, behold, I bring you good tidings of great joy, which shall be to all people. For unto you is born this day in the city of David a Saviour, which is Christ the Lord"* (Luke 2:8-11).

Surely, the fact that Jesus being the eternal Son of God was born as a member of the human race was a cause for rejoicing, but the angels may also rejoice over the birth of other babies as well.

One of the most precious pictures presented in the life and ministry of Jesus is found when Jesus called a little child to Himself and used that child as an example to others.

> *"And Jesus called a little child unto him, and set him in the midst of them, And said, Verily I say unto you, Except ye be converted, and become as little children, ye shall not*

*enter into the kingdom of heaven. Whosoever therefore
shall humble himself as this little child, the same is greatest
in the kingdom of heaven"* (Matthew 18:2-4).

As Jesus warned His listeners about how they should treat
the little children, He made an interesting statement about the
relationship of angels to the little ones. *"Take heed that ye despise
not one of these little ones; for I say unto you, That in heaven their
angels do always behold the face of my Father which is in heaven"*
(Matthew 18:10). If the little ones have 'their angels', then one
must be assigned to them at birth. I can imagine the angels
rejoicing each time a baby is born.

The same angels rejoice each time that a sinner is born
again. *"Likewise, I say unto you, there is joy in the presence of the
angels of God over one sinner that repenteth"* (Luke 15:10). From
the time that a soul is saved, God commissions an angel (or
angels) to be a guardian over him. *"Are they not all ministering
spirits, sent forth to minister for them who shall be heirs of salvation?"* (Hebrews 1:14).

While the angels have done a lot of rejoicing, they
have unfortunately observed some events that must have
brought them a lot of grief. In fact, it was one of their own
who was the cause of great judgment falling on a beautiful
creation.

The condition of the original earth did not remain in its
beautiful and pristine condition because one of the angels
(Lucifer) who originally rejoiced at the creation of the earth
brought destruction when he left his habitation and dared to
believe that he could become equal with God. Dr. Erich Sauer
from Germany was one of the greatest writers of the twentieth

century and he described what happened to the perfect earth as God reacted to Lucifer's rebellion.

> With the fall of Satan there must have been associated the ruin of the region over which he ruled, as is evidenced by the organic connexion between spirit and nature, and by the later and resembling fall of man, though this last to a smaller extent (Genesis 3:18). World and earth catastrophes occurred as counter-workings of the righteousness of God against this cosmic revolt. The creation was subjected to vanity (Romans 8:20, 21).

> All details are hidden from our knowledge. Only this is certain, that death and destruction in the world of plants and animals raged on the earth for unthinkable periods long before the race of man. This is proved very clearly by the geological strata and the stages of the development of the prehistoric animal world. The strata of the earth beneath us are simply "a huge cemetery that is enclosed in its stony field." Indeed many rapacious beasts of the prehistoric time were terrible monsters with the most voracious and deadly power of destruction.[76]

An earth that was touched by sin still remained as a home for many creatures of various types for a very long time as revealed by archaeological and paleontological discoveries. Thus, the seed of sin and death that had come to earth did not prevent it from being a home to those who dwelt upon it.

The seed of sin and death also dwells in every baby that is born into Adam's family. The Psalmist David was not born out of wedlock, but he still acknowledged that he was conceived in sin: *"Behold, I was shapen in iniquity; and in sin did my mother conceive me"* (Psalm 51:5). It does not take long for sin to reveal itself in a newborn baby who learns very quickly that if he screams loud enough he will get attention, even if he feels no pain or hunger. *"The wicked are estranged from the womb: they go astray as soon as they be born, speaking lies"* (Psalm 58:3). It is not just the personal sins of that child as it grows up that will eventually bring condemnation, however, it is the depraved nature that was inherited from Adam: *"Wherefore, as by one man sin entered into the world, and death by sin; and so death passed upon all men, for that all have sinned"* (Romans 5:12), and *"For as in Adam all die"* (1 Corinthians 15:22a).

The earth continued in its sinful state for possibly millions or billions of years before the judgment of God brought it to become an uninhabitable place. Likewise, the child grows up in an innocent condition until God holds him accountable for his sins through the conviction of the Holy Spirit.

The Dead Earth

The ultimate affects from God's judgment on what had once been a beautiful and vibrant earth is revealed: *"And the earth was without form, and void; and darkness was upon the face of the deep. And the Spirit of God moved upon the face of the waters"* (Genesis 1:2). It was an earth that was void of life as darkness had covered it removing any warmth from the sun, probably bringing on the ice age. The God who had originally created it to the rejoicing of angels (Job 38:7) is the same One who had brought the judgment. *"When I made the cloud the garment thereof, and thick darkness a swaddlingband for it"* (Job 38:9). The description of the earth at that point in time is a picture of the child that grows up to feel the convicting power of God's Holy Spirit.

Whereas Romans 5:12 and 1 Corinthians 15:22a above both reveal that Adam's sin brought death upon all the human race, the Apostle Paul repeatedly reminded those who had been saved that they were spiritually dead prior to being made alive in Jesus Christ.

"For if through the offence of one many be dead, much more the grace of God, and the gift by grace, which is by one man, Jesus Christ, hath abounded unto many" (Romans 5:15)

"And you hath he quickened, who were dead in trespasses and sins — Even when we were dead in sins, hath quickened us together with Christ, (by grace ye are saved;)" (Ephesians 2:1, 5)

"And you, being dead in your sins and the uncircumcision of your flesh, hath he quickened together with him, having forgiven you all trespasses" (Colossians 2:13)

"But she that liveth in pleasure is dead while she liveth" (1 Timothy 5:6)

"For the wages of sin is death—" (Romans 6:23a)

A child becomes spiritually dead and separated from God at the point of conviction when he becomes accountable for his sins, and must believe in Jesus Christ to receive the life that can only come from Him. *"He that hath the Son hath life; and he that hath not the Son of God hath not life"* (1 John 5:12). It is no wonder that Jesus told Nicodemus, *"Ye must be born again"* (John 3:7). It is also significant that Nicodemus came in the darkness of night with a heart filled with spiritual darkness.

The Bible describes the person who is not saved as being not only dead, but also dwelling in darkness. *"For ye were sometimes darkness, but now are ye light in the Lord: walk as children of light"* (Ephesians 5:8). After Jesus told Nicodemus those beautiful words found in John 3:16-18, He then described the sad decision that too many people make: *"And this is the condemnation, that light is come into the world, and men loved darkness rather than light, because their deeds were evil"* (John 3:19). The life style of those who choose to live in darkness is revealed in Scripture.

> *"He that saith he is in the light, and hateth his brother, is in darkness even until now. He that loveth his brother abideth in the light, and there is none occasion of stumbling in him. But he that hateth his brother is in darkness, and walketh in darkness, and knoweth not whither he goeth, because that darkness hath blinded his eyes"* (1 John 2:9-11)

The unbelieving Jews were always against Jesus and opposed all of His teachings. Jesus explained their unbelief by quoting Isaiah 6:10 which spoke of their spiritual blindness.

> *"Therefore they could not believe, because that Esaias said again, He hath blinded their eyes, and hardened their heart; that they should not see with their eyes, nor understand with their heart, and be converted, and I should heal them"* (John 12:39, 40)

The earth without form and void was dwelling in physical darkness and death. The lost soul is dwelling in spiritual darkness and death. The parallel is undeniable!

The Recreated Earth

The old earth was reformed in the six days work to once again become a beautiful place prepared for the habitation of a new creation. The seeds and plants that had once grown freely on the previous earth had been dormant in the period of darkness they had endured. The light that came on the first day (possibly from the Shekinah glory from the presence of the Lord) brought warmth back to the surface of the earth. After He had made the firmament (atmosphere) on the second day, God caused the dry land to appear and commanded that grass and trees begin to grow on the third day.

> *"And God said, Let the earth bring forth grass, the herb yielding seed, and the fruit tree yielding fruit after his kind, whose seed is in itself, upon the earth: and it was so. And the earth brought forth grass, and herb yielding seed after his kind, and the tree yielding fruit, whose seed was in itself, after his kind: and God saw that it was good. And the evening and the morning were the third day"* (Genesis 1:11-13)

You will notice that the seed was already *"in itself, upon the earth."* There is no implication that they were created at this time, but perhaps left over and preserved from the original creation and only allowed to grow again. On the fourth day, the sun and moon were ordained to provide warmth and light and bring signs, seasons, days and years (Genesis 1:14-19). The earth was then ready for a new creation!

On the fifth day, God created all the fowls of the air and creatures to dwell in the sea (Genesis 1:20-23). On the sixth day, He created all the creatures to live on land and then Adam was His final creative act (Genesis 1:24-27). God looked upon all He had made in the six days and declared it to be 'very good' (Genesis 1:31).

God was able to rest on the seventh day from all He had 'created' and 'made'. He had 'made' the earth to be everything that would be needed for all the life He had 'created'. It was a perfect and beautiful earth to be a habitation for perfect creatures.

All those who have rejected God's offer of salvation stand before God in spiritual darkness and death. Only the coming of the Lord Jesus Christ could offer any light and hope for such a condition. *"The people which sat in darkness saw great light; and to them which sat in the region and shadow of death light is sprung up"* (Matthew 4:16).

God created man in His own image as one who is triune – body, soul, and spirit. While the spirit is the part of man that can have fellowship with God, the body relates to the earth and the soul is related to other living beings. A lost individual has no fellowship with God since he is spiritually dead, but the body and soul are still alive and active. It is the soul that is the seat of personality which contains intellect, emotions, and will. God has designed the plan of salvation whereby the gospel appeals to the intellect to be believed. The Holy Spirit uses the gospel message to bring conviction: *"Now when they heard this, they were pricked in their heart, and said unto Peter and to the rest of the apostles, Men and brethren, what shall we do?"* (Acts 2:37). The unsaved person must then exercise his will to believe the saving message of Jesus Christ: *"Then Peter said unto them, Repent, and be baptized every one of you in the name of Jesus Christ for the remission of sins, and ye shall receive the gift of the Holy Ghost"* (Acts 2:38). When the sinner comes to Jesus in faith and repentance he is born again spiritually and becomes a child of God. It is then that he becomes a new creation in an old body. *"Therefore if any man be in Christ, he is a new creature: old things are passed away; behold, all things are become new"* (2 Corinthians 5:17).

While the reader may question the comparisons that I have made between the earth and a lost soul, it should be noted that the Apostle Paul presented the same truth: *"For God, who commanded the light to shine out of darkness, hath shined in our hearts, to give the light of the knowledge of the glory of God in the face of Jesus Christ"* (2 Corinthians 4:6). There can be no doubt that his reference to the *"God who commanded the light to shine out of darkness"* is referring to Genesis 1:3 and He is presented as the same One who shined in the darkness of our hearts! How He gives light to a sin darkened heart is of great significance.

In the Old Testament, the Word of God is described as a light: *"Thy word is a lamp unto my feet, and a light unto my path"* (Psalm 119:105), and *"The entrance of thy words giveth light; it giveth understanding unto the simple"* (Psalm 119:130). In the New Testament, it is the gospel of Jesus Christ that gives light to the unsaved heart.

When Jesus saved Saul of Tarsus, He explained to him the special ministry he had been called to perform. Saul had already become the Apostle Paul when he shared with King Agrippa what the Lord had commanded.

"Rise, and stand upon thy feet: for I have appeared unto thee for this purpose, to make thee a minister and a witness both of these things which thou hast seen, and of those things in the which I will appear unto thee; Delivering thee from the people, and from the Gentiles, unto whom now I send thee, <u>To open their eyes, and to turn them from darkness to light</u>, *and from the power of Satan unto God, that they may receive forgiveness of sins, and inheritance among them which are sanctified by faith that is in me"* (Acts 26:16-18) (Emphasis mine)

It was the preaching of the gospel of Jesus Christ that would produce that light: *"That Christ should suffer, and that he should be the first that should rise from the dead, and should show light unto the people, and to the Gentiles"* (Acts 26:23).

When a sinner receives Jesus Christ, a sin darkened heart is illuminated by the light of the glorious gospel and he is transformed into a saint of God.

"Who hath delivered us from the power of darkness, and hath translated us into the kingdom of his dear Son" (Colossians 1:13)

"But ye are a chosen generation, a royal priesthood, an holy nation, a peculiar people; that ye should show forth the praises of him who hath called you out of darkness into his marvellous light" (1 Peter 2:9)

Unfortunately, not every unsaved person who hears the gospel will believe and be saved. The devil does everything he can to cause the unsaved to reject the gospel to keep him in the darkness of his evil kingdom.

"But if our gospel be hid, it is hid to them that are lost: In whom the god of this world hath blinded the minds of them which believe not, lest the light of the glorious gospel of Christ, who is the image of God, should shine unto them" (2 Corinthians 4:3, 4)

But, those who do accept the Gospel receive many benefits from the Lord!

The darkness that once dwelt in the lost person's heart had also brought spiritual death. But, the entrance of light also brings spiritual life. That life is not only a gift from Christ, but it is the very life of Christ living in the believer. It is a life that is called both eternal and everlasting – a life that will never end!

"but the gift of God is eternal life through Jesus Christ our Lord" (Romans 6:23b)

"He that believeth on the Son hath everlasting life: and he that believeth not the Son shall not see life; but the wrath of God abideth on him" (John 3:36)

"Verily, verily, I say unto you, He that heareth my word, and believeth on him that sent me, hath everlasting life, and shall not come into condemnation; but is passed from death unto life" (John 5:24)

"And this is the record, that God hath given to us eternal life, and this life is in his Son. He that hath the Son hath life; and he that hath not the Son of God hath not life" (1 John 5:11, 12)

With Jesus living in the heart of the believer, the body literally becomes a temple (dwelling place) of the Holy Spirit. It is not only a dwelling place for Him, but it is a house that He owns!

"Know ye not that ye are the temple of God, and that the Spirit of God dwelleth in you?" (1 Corinthians 3:16)

"What? know ye not that your body is the temple of the Holy Ghost which is in you, which ye have of God, and ye are not your own? For ye are bought with a price: therefore glorify God in your body, and in your spirit, which are God's" (1 Corinthians 6:19, 20)

When God completed His six day's work, the earth was absolutely beautiful and perfect in every way. When His work of redemption is completed, the child of God stands before Him just as perfect and precious. The new born soul can sing the precious words found in the grand old hymn written by Charles A. Tindley.

NOTHING BETWEEN

Nothing between my soul and my Savior,
Naught of this world's delusive dream;
I have renounced all sinful pleasure;
Jesus is mine, there's nothing between.

Nothing between, like worldly pleasure;
Habits of life, though harmless they seem;
Must not my heart from Him ever sever;
He is my all, there's nothing between.

Nothing between, like pride or station;
Self or friends shall not intervene;
Though it may cost me much tribulation,
I am resolved, there's nothing between.

Nothing between, e'en many hard trials,
Though the whole world against me convene;
Watching with prayer and much self denial,
I'll triumph at last, there's nothing between.

How wonderful it would be if every Christian could remain in that condition! But, alas, as surely as innocence was broken in the Garden, sin will soon be committed by the body of the new Christian that will affect fellowship with God. When Adam sinned, the earth and all its creatures would be affected, but God was not through. Thank God that He is not through with us when we allow sin to come into our lives!

The Cursed Earth

God told Adam that if he ate of the forbidden tree that he would surely die. There is no biblical evidence that he was warned about what else would happen. One can only imagine how Adam felt when God pronounced His curse on not only Adam, but also the entire earth and every other creature that dwelt on it.

> "And the LORD God said unto the serpent, Because thou hast done this, thou art cursed above all cattle, and above every beast of the field; upon thy belly shalt thou go, and dust shalt thou eat all the days of thy life: And I will put enmity between thee and the woman, and between thy seed and her seed; it shall bruise thy head, and thou shalt

bruise his heel. Unto the woman he said, I will greatly multiply thy sorrow and thy conception; in sorrow thou shalt bring forth children; and thy desire shall be to thy husband, and he shall rule over thee. And unto Adam he said, Because thou hast hearkened unto the voice of thy wife, and hast eaten of the tree, of which I commanded thee, saying, Thou shalt not eat of it: cursed is the ground for thy sake; in sorrow shalt thou eat of it all the days of thy life; Thorns also and thistles shall it bring forth to thee; and thou shalt eat the herb of the field; In the sweat of thy face shalt thou eat bread, till thou return unto the ground; for out of it wast thou taken: for dust thou art, and unto dust shalt thou return" (Genesis 3:14-19)

God did not destroy the earth with all its life, but He placed a curse that would plague them as long as the earth endured.

All the floods, earthquakes, storms, volcanoes, droughts, tsunamis, etc., that we have experienced can be traced back to this curse. Yet God has continued to provide the earth as not only a dwelling place for all His creatures, but a beautiful planet in a glorious universe. One day, however, this present earth will be destroyed. *"But the heavens and the earth, which are now, by the same word are kept in store, reserved unto fire against the day of judgment and perdition of ungodly men"* (2 Peter 3:7). God's dealings with the earth are once again a picture that presents the way God deals with the soul that has been saved.

When a Christian sins, it is committed by the body and is not charged against the soul and spirit which remain perfect. *"Whosoever is born of God doth not commit sin; for his seed remaineth in him: and he cannot sin, because he is born of God"*

(1 John 3:9). It is the soul and spirit that are born again, not the body!

If the sins committed by the body are confessed, they are forgiven and fellowship with God is not broken. The same blood that was used to save us will also bring forgiveness to restore our communion with God.

> *"If we say that we have fellowship with him, and walk in darkness, we lie, and do not the truth: But if we walk in the light, as he is in the light, we have fellowship one with another, and the blood of Jesus Christ his Son cleanseth us from all sin. If we say that we have no sin, we deceive ourselves, and the truth is not in us. If we confess our sins, he is faithful and just to forgive us our sins, and to cleanse us from all unrighteousness. If we say that we have not sinned, we make him a liar, and his word is not in us"* (1 John 1:6-10)

It is unfortunate that most Christians allow sins to dwell in their bodies from time to time without confessing them to God. In such cases, God has promised to chasten the body just as a loving father is supposed to do to his children.

> *"Behold, happy is the man whom God correcteth: therefore despise not thou the chastening of the Almighty"* (Job 5:17)

> *"My son, despise not the chastening of the LORD; neither be weary of his correction: For whom the LORD loveth he correcteth; even as a father the son in whom he delighteth"* (Proverbs 3:11, 12)

"And ye have forgotten the exhortation which speaketh unto you as unto children, My son, despise not thou the chastening of the Lord, nor faint when thou art rebuked of him: For whom the Lord loveth he chasteneth, and scourgeth every son whom he receiveth. If ye endure chastening, God dealeth with you as with sons; for what son is he whom the father chasteneth not?" (Hebrews 12:5-7)

His chastening is always administered out of love and is not designed to just make us suffer, but to return us to fellowship with Him and fruitfulness in our service for Him. *"Now no chastening for the present seemeth to be joyous, but grievous: nevertheless afterward it yieldeth the peaceable fruit of righteousness unto them which are exercised thereby"* (Hebrews 12:11). Regardless of whether or not the Christian is living in fellowship with God, he still endures the difficulty of having an eternal soul and spirit dwelling in a body that is destined to die. The Apostle Paul often wrote of the turmoil that goes on with a new creation living in an old body.

"For I reckon that the sufferings of this present time are not worthy to be compared with the glory which shall be revealed in us. For the earnest expectation of the creature waiteth for the manifestation of the sons of God. For the creature was made subject to vanity, not willingly, but by reason of him who hath subjected the same in hope, Because the creature itself also shall be delivered from the bondage of corruption into the glorious liberty of the children of God. For we know that the whole creation groaneth and travaileth in pain together until now. And not only they, but ourselves also, which have the firstfruits of the Spirit, even we ourselves groan within ourselves,

waiting for the adoption, to wit, the redemption of our body" (Romans 8:18-23)

"Always bearing about in the body the dying of the Lord Jesus, that the life also of Jesus might be made manifest in our body. For we which live are alway delivered unto death for Jesus' sake, that the life also of Jesus might be made manifest in our mortal flesh" (2 Corinthians 4:10, 11)

While Paul was grieving over this conflict within him, he rejoiced over the assurance that one day his body would be redeemed to be as perfect and sinless as his inner man. Until then, he would live a life of victory through the power of God. *"O wretched man that I am! who shall deliver me from the body of this death? I thank God through Jesus Christ our Lord. So then with the mind I myself serve the law of God; but with the flesh the law of sin"* (Romans 7:24, 25). We should do no less!

This cursed earth is destined to one day be destroyed and our cursed body will one day become "dust and ashes" and return to the earth that Adam was taken from: *"for dust thou art, and unto dust shalt thou return"* (Genesis 3:19f).

It is difficult to imagine anyone who suffered more than Job. In the time of his affliction, he constantly wrote about the future of his body.

"And why dost thou not pardon my transgression, and take away mine iniquity? for now shall I sleep in the dust; and thou shalt seek me in the morning, but I shall not be" (Job 7:21)

"Remember, I beseech thee, that thou hast made me as the clay; and wilt thou bring me into dust again?" (Job 10:9)

"And where is now my hope? as for my hope, who shall see it? They shall go down to the bars of the pit, when our rest together is in the dust" (Job 17:15, 16)

"One dieth in his full strength, being wholly at ease and quiet. His breasts are full of milk, and his bones are moistened with marrow. And another dieth in the bitterness of his soul, and never eateth with pleasure. They shall lie down alike in the dust, and the worms shall cover them" (Job 21:23-26)

While he was aware that his body would one day return to the dust, he also knew that it would not remain in the dust. *"For I know that my redeemer liveth, and that he shall stand at the latter day upon the earth: And though after my skin worms destroy this body, yet in my flesh shall I see God"* (Job 19:25, 26)

Solomon in all his wisdom wrote throughout the book of Ecclesiastes about man living under the sun. He also revealed what the end of man's life on earth would involve.

"All go unto one place; all are of the dust, and all turn to dust again" (Ecclesiastes 3:20)

"Then shall the dust return to the earth as it was: and the spirit shall return unto God who gave it" (Ecclesiastes 12:7)

We live in the land of the dying and must die to go to the land the living! Our bodies are living under the curse of death yet they can still be used to bring glory to God because of the new life which is within us.

> *"Let not sin therefore reign in your mortal body, that ye should obey it in the lusts thereof. Neither yield ye your members as instruments of unrighteousness unto sin: but yield yourselves unto God, as those that are alive from the dead, and your members as instruments of righteousness unto God"* (Romans 6:12, 13)

This earth is cursed and destined to be destroyed yet it will still bring glory to God. The wrath of God that will be poured out in the Great Tribulation period will bring cataclysms and catastrophes to the earth as evidently happened before the six days work. There will be darkness over the earth as the sun and moon refuse to shine (Zephaniah 1:15; Joel 3:15; Revelation 16:10). The earth will begin to quake and tremble in the midst of that darkness (Joel 2:10; Revelation 6:12, 16:18). Mountains and islands will be moved out of their places (Revelation 6:14, 8:8, 16:20). Stars (or asteroids) will begin to fall upon the earth (Revelation 6:13). Jesus said that if these things are allowed to continue no life will be left on earth (Matthew 24:22). It will appear that the sin of Adam and Eve will cause the earth to once again be 'without form and void' just as Lucifer's sin had previously done. But, it will not reach that condition because Jesus will come in glory and His presence will bring an end to the judgments. Then, He will institute His kingdom and the earth will know peace. *"For the earth shall be filled with the knowledge of the glory of the LORD, as the waters cover the sea"* (Habakkuk 2:14). God always has and always will receive glory from the earth regardless of what it goes through.

Our cursed bodies are destined to the dust (if Jesus does not come first) but they can still be used to bring glory to God when we allow the light that is within us to shine to those who are around us. *"Let your light so shine before men, that they may see your good works, and glorify your Father which is in heaven"* (Matthew 5:16). God can use anything that happens to our bodies to further the outreach of His gospel. *"But I would ye should understand, brethren, that the things which happened unto me have fallen out rather unto the furtherance of the gospel"* (Philippians 1:12). So, we need to have the attitude and desire of the Apostle Paul: *"Christ shall be magnified in my body, whether it be by life, or by death"* (Philippians 1:20f).

Thank God that He has not yet finished His final work with the earth and He has not completed His final work in our bodies!

The Eternal Earth

Geologists tell us that many catastrophes occurred on the earth millions or billions of years ago. They have discovered evidence that cause them to believe that mountain ranges were moved out of their places and entire areas were folded together as one would fold a piece of paper. What was once on the surface is now found deep within the earth. Fossil remains are found revealing that various creatures lived at different times and many of them are now found buried at successive levels in the earth. Whatever happened was not a natural occurrence, but the judgment of God that came upon the earth while Satan was trying to keep it under control. God's judgments left the earth as a dead and dark planet that was without form and void as described in Genesis 1:2. God could have left it in that condition, but He had other plans!

In the six days work, God did another mighty act of taking the earth and once again making it a beautiful planet to be inhabited by a new creation. But, Adam's sin brought another curse on it. God revealed in His Word that earth and its atmosphere (the heaven around it) would remain in that condition until the day when He would totally destroy it. He further promised that He would create a new heaven and earth that would be eternally righteous and never have to bear a curse.

> *"For, behold, I create new heavens and a new earth: and the former shall not be remembered, nor come into mind"* (Isaiah 65:17)

> *"But the day of the Lord will come as a thief in the night; in the which the heavens shall pass away with a great noise, and the elements shall melt with fervent heat, the earth also and the works that are therein shall be burned up"* (2 Peter 3:10)

> *"Nevertheless we, according to his promise, look for new heavens and a new earth, wherein dwelleth righteousness"* (2 Peter 3:13)

This destruction of the old heaven and old earth will probably take place while the Lord is judging all the ungodly at the Great White Throne Judgment. *"And I saw a great white throne, and him that sat on it, <u>from whose face the earth and the heaven fled away; and there was found no place for them</u>"* (Revelation 20:11) (Emphasis mine). At the conclusion of that judgment, the Apostle John was allowed to see the new heaven and earth. *"And I saw a new heaven and a new earth: for the first heaven and the first earth were passed away; and there was no more sea"* (Revelation 21:1).

The God who will create a new and eternal earth also has a plan for the bodies of His own, whether they are still living at the coming of the Lord or if they have died and returned to the dust.

> *"Behold, I show you a mystery; We shall not all sleep, but we shall all be changed, In a moment, in the twinkling of an eye, at the last trump: for the trumpet shall sound, and the dead shall be raised incorruptible, and we shall be changed. For this corruptible must put on incorruption, and this mortal must put on immortality. So when this corruptible shall have put on incorruption, and this mortal shall have put on immortality, then shall be brought to pass the saying that is written, Death is swallowed up in victory"* (1 Corinthians 15:51-54)

> *"For this we say unto you by the word of the Lord, that we which are alive and remain unto the coming of the Lord shall not prevent them which are asleep. For the Lord himself shall descend from heaven with a shout, with the voice of the archangel, and with the trump of God: and the dead in Christ shall rise first: Then we which are*

alive and remain shall be caught up together with them in the clouds, to meet the Lord in the air: and so shall we ever be with the Lord" (1 Thessalonians 4:15-17)

These new bodies will be both immortal and incorruptible revealing that they will be everlasting and never know the stain of sin or the sentence of death. They will also be glorious just like the resurrected body of Jesus.

"As for me, I will behold thy face in righteousness: I shall be satisfied, when I awake, with thy likeness" (Psalm 17:15)

"For our conversation is in heaven; from whence also we look for the Saviour, the Lord Jesus Christ: Who shall change our vile body, that it may be fashioned like unto his glorious body, according to the working whereby he is able even to subdue all things unto himself" (Philippians 3:20, 21)

"Beloved, now are we the sons of God, and it doth not yet appear what we shall be: but we know that, when he shall appear, we shall be like him; for we shall see him as he is" (1 John 3:2)

After receiving these glorified bodies, all of God's children will be finally perfect and sinless – body, soul, and spirit. *"And the very God of peace sanctify you wholly; and I pray God your whole spirit and soul and body be preserved blameless unto the coming of our Lord Jesus Christ"* (1 Thessalonians 5:23)!

God has special plans for His glorified people on His newly created heaven and earth. He allowed the Apostle John to see what will take place as they are brought together.

"And I John saw the holy city, new Jerusalem, coming down from God out of heaven, prepared as a bride adorned for her husband. And I heard a great voice out of heaven saying, Behold, the tabernacle of God is with men, and he will dwell with them, and they shall be his people, and God himself shall be with them, and be their God. And God shall wipe away all tears from their eyes; and there shall be no more death, neither sorrow, nor crying, neither shall there be any more pain: for the former things are passed away. And he that sat upon the throne said, Behold, I make all things new. And he said unto me, Write: for these words are true and faithful" (Revelation 21:2-5)

The new earth and its inhabitants will not only be perfect at that point in time, but God has promised that no sin will ever defile that beautiful city or the people that dwell in it. *"And there shall in no wise enter into it any thing that defileth, neither whatsoever worketh abomination, or maketh a lie: but they which are written in the Lamb's book of life"* (Revelation 21:27). Thus, the Bible concludes with a perfect people dwelling on a perfect earth in the presence of a holy God.

"And he showed me a pure river of water of life, clear as crystal, proceeding out of the throne of God and of the Lamb. In the midst of the street of it, and on either side of the river, was there the tree of life, which bare twelve manner of fruits, and yielded her fruit every month: and the leaves of the tree were for the healing of the nations. And

there shall be no more curse: but the throne of God and of the Lamb shall be in it; and his servants shall serve him: And they shall see his face; and his name shall be in their foreheads. And there shall be no night there; and they need no candle, neither light of the sun; for the Lord God giveth them light: and they shall reign for ever and ever" (Revelation 22:1-5)

This description is similar to the original Garden of Eden before it was defiled by the sin of Adam and Eve.

༒

Details about the earth are given from the first verse of Genesis to the last chapters of Revelation. Since the primary purpose of the Bible is to present God's provision of redemption for the fallen of Adam's race, it should be expected that everything included in the Bible somehow pictures salvation. Therefore, the history and future of the earth picture in detail the life of a person who accepts Jesus as Savior from his birth to eternity. This comparison can only be made if the "Ruin To Restoration" theory of creation is true.

The original creation of the earth was perfect and innocent like a new born baby. The earth in a condition of being without form and void was a dark and dead planet and is similar to the spiritual condition of one who is lost. The beautiful earth with its new life at the end of the six days work was like a person who has just been born again. The earth going through judgment after the sin of Adam and Eve is similar to the body of the Christian being chastened because of his sins. The earth and every Christian will one day be glorified and perfected forever. The comparison is undeniable!

Thus, God's creation story presents the story of salvation. God provided all of creation and He provides all of salvation: *"Salvation is of the LORD"* (Jonah 2:9). There would have never been a creation without Him and no one would ever be saved without Him! That's why we call Him 'Creator' and that's why we call Him 'Savior'!

While it is unfortunate that many deny His work in creation and accept the theory of evolution, it is absolutely tragic that many reject His offer of salvation! Some reject Him because they claim to be atheists. Some are depending on religion or their own good works and will not place their faith in Jesus Christ. Others take pleasure in their sins and refuse the repentance that is needed to bring them to salvation. Whatever the reason (or reasons) may be, they are separated from God and will never know peace or have the privilege of dwelling in the new heaven and new earth unless they accept Jesus.

Please allow me to have a personal word with the unsaved. If you are like most people, you have faced a lot of problems on this earth and will most likely face many more. Some of those problems have come about because of your own sins and failures, but many were brought about by the curse placed on the earth – storms, hurricanes, tornadoes, earthquakes, blizzards, volcanoes, droughts, disease, etc. The curse placed on Adam's race has resulted in the death of some of your loved ones. With all the problems you may have already endured, I can promise you that without Jesus those were the best times you will ever know. Things will only get worse here and in eternity!

If you accept Jesus as your Savior, you will still have problems as you live in a cursed body on a cursed earth, but you will never have to go through anything alone. While you are living in a body destined for death, you will know that you have a soul and spirit that are bound for heaven. You will also be able to rejoice in knowing that one day you will have a glorified body living on a new earth and will enjoy spending eternity with the Lord and other people who are just like you.

Hopefully, you will have many more good days than bad ones and more times filled with laughter than with weeping. You will have the privilege of seeing many beautiful sunsets and many nights of gazing upon the beauty of the stars as they declare the glory of God (Psalm 19:1). You may have the pleasure of walking on fresh fallen snow in the winter and then seeing new life appear in the springtime. There are so many gorgeous sites on earth that you may be able to visit during your journey here. Through it all you will know that the One who created and made it all is the same One who loves you so much that He went to the cross of Calvary and died in your place just because He wants to spend eternity with you. As you gaze upon what He did in creation and think of all He did to save your soul, it should cause you to want to glorify Him as your Creator and Savior!

Our eyes have seen some wonderful sights and our ears have heard some wonderful things, but nothing here compares to the eternity He is creating for us.

"But as it is written, Eye hath not seen, nor ear heard, neither have entered into the heart of man, the things which

God hath prepared for them that love him" (1 Corinthians 2:9)

"And if children, then heirs; heirs of God, and joint-heirs with Christ; if so be that we suffer with him, that we may be also glorified together. For I reckon that the sufferings of this present time are not worthy to be compared with the glory which shall be revealed in us" (Romans 8:17, 18)

You don't want to miss His salvation or you will never be able to enjoy His greatest creation! This present creation does provide a picture of salvation. His great salvation will one day provide you with an eternal and perfect creation.

ENDNOTES

Chapter 1 – In The Beginning

[1] Dr. Clarence Larkin, Dispensational Truth, (Rev. Clarence Larkin Est., 1918), p. 21
[2] Dr. Harold E. Cooper, *A Whisper Of His Ways*, (Baptist Trumpet, 1975), p. 24
[3] John C. Whitcomb and Henry M. Morris, *The Genesis Flood*, (Presbyterian and Reformed Publishing Company, 1961), pp. 477, 478
[4] Ibid, p. 126

Chapter 3 – What Earth Has To Say

[5] John C. Whitcomb and Henry M. Morris, *The Genesis Flood*, (Presbyterian and Reformed Publishing Company, 1961), p. 240
[6] Answers In Genesis, "Arguments We Think Creationists Should NOT use", http://www/answersingenesis.org/home/area/faq/don't_use.asp
[7] John C. Whitcomb and Henry M. Morris, *The Genesis Flood*, (Presbyterian and Reformed Publishing Company, 1961), p. 241
[8] Ibid., p. 139
[9] Ibid., p. 201
[10] Ibid., pp. 214-216

11 Ibid., p. 264

12 Dr. John Morris, "Why Did God Give The Rainbow Sign?" (Institute of Creation Research), http:///www.icr.org/article/2598/Dr.John'sQ&A/Why Did God Give The Rainbow Sign?-Ins

13 The World Book Encyclopedia (Field Enterprises Educational Corporation, 1970)

14 John C. Whitcomb and Henry M. Morris, *The Genesis Flood*, (Presbyterian and Reformed Publishing Company, 1961), pp. 144, 145

15 Ibid., p. 203

16 Ibid., p. 157

17 Ibid., p. 419

18 J. L. Kirby: "Flood Geology", *Journal of the American Scientific Affiliation*, January 2950, p. 10

19 C. A. Arnold: *An Introduction To Paleobotany* (New York, McGraw-Hill, 1947), p. 24

20 John C. Whitcomb and Henry M. Morris, *The Genesis Flood*, (Presbyterian and Reformed Publishing Company, 1961), p. 419

21 Ibid., pp. 162, 163

22 Ibid., pp. 434, 435

23 Ibid., p. 369

24 Answers in Genesis http:///www.aig/org/articles/2007/06/01/reason-seven-supernova-1987a

25 Answers In Genesis http:///www.aig/org/ti/i2/cosmology.asp

26 John C. Whitcomb and Henry M. Morris, *The Genesis Flood*, (Presbyterian and Reformed Publishing Company, 1961), p. 293

27 Ibid., p. 305

28 Dr. John Morris, "Why Did God Give The Rainbow Sign?" (Institute of Creation Research), http:///www.

icr.org/article/2598/Dr.John'sQ&A/Why Did God Give The Rainbow Sign?-Ins

29 Wallace S. Broeker, Mauriace Ewing and Bruce C. Heezen: "Evidence for an Abrupt Change In Climate Close to 11,000 Years Ago," American Journal of Science, Vol. 258, June 1960, p. 441

30 John C. Whitcomb and Henry M. Morris, *The Genesis Flood*, (Presbyterian and Reformed Publishing Company, 1961), p. 376

31 Ibid., p. 346

32 Ibid., p. 343

33 Dinosaur Floor: Meet The Dinosaurs, *The Age Of The Dinosaurs*, http://www.cotf.edu/ete/modules/meses/dinosaurflr/meet.html

34 FoxNews.Com, "Fossils Challenge Old Evolution Theory", August 9, 2007
http://www.foxnews.com/printer_friendly_wires/2007Aug09/0,4675

35 Discovery Health News, "Neanderthal DNA Shows No Interbreeding With Humans", Nov. 15, 2006, http://health.discovery.com/news/healthscout/article.html

36 John C. Whitcomb and Henry M. Morris, *The Genesis Flood*, (Presbyterian and Reformed Publishing Company, 1961), p. xvii

Chapter 6 – Answering The Critics

37 Dr. Kent Hovind and Stephen Lawwell, *The Gap Theory*, (Creation Science Evangelism, February, 2005) Preface

38 Ibid., p. 18

39 Ibid., p. 4

40 Answers In Genesis, http:///www.aig/org/articles/nab/gap-ruin-reconstruction-theories

41 Erich Sauer, *The Dawn Of World Redemptio*n, (Wm. B. Eerdmans Publishing Company), pp. 35, 36

42 A Long Held View, http://www.creationdays.dk/withoutformandvoid/1.html

43 Louis Ginsberg, *"The Legends of the Jews"*, (Jewish Publications Soc. of America, Phila., 1954, Vol. 1, p. 4.

44 A Long Held View, http://www.creationdays.dk/withoutformandvoid/1.html

45 Caedmon, "Genesis: Excursus All, translated from the Old English by Lawrence Mason, in the "Yale Studies in English" series edited by Albert S. Cook, Henry Holt, N. Y., 1915, lines 14-35, 68, 79, 80, 92f, 114

46 D. F. Payne, *"Genesis One Reconsidered"*, (Tyndale Press, London, 1964) p. 7 fn

47 A Long Held View, http://www.creationdays.dk/withoutformandvoid/1.html

48 Dr. Kent Hovind and Stephen Lawwell, *The Gap Theory*, (Creation Science Evangelism, February, 2005), p. 6

49 Delitzsch, Franz, *"New Commentary on Genesis"*, Clark, Edinburgh, 1888, Vol., p. 79

50 The Gap Theory, http://www.drdino.com/QandA/index.jsp, page 4

51 Ibid, p. 5

52 Gap Ruin Restoration Theories, http://www.Aig/org/articles/nab/gap-ruin-reconstruction-theories

53 Ibid,

54 Dr. Kent Hovind and Stephen Lawwell, *The Gap Theory*, (Creation Science Evangelism, February, 2005), p. 10

55 Gap Ruin Restoration Theories, http://www.Aig/org/articles/nab/gap-ruin-reconstruction-theories

[56] Dr. Kent Hovind and Stephen Lawwell, *The Gap Theory*, (Creation Science Evangelism, February, 2005), pp. 19, 20

[57] Death Before Sin?, http://www.icr.org/article/3367/

[58] Gap Ruin Restoration Theories, http://www.Aig/org/articles/nab/gap-ruin-reconstruction-theories

[59] Dr. Kent Hovind and Stephen Lawwell, *The Gap Theory*, (Creation Science Evangelism, February, 2005), pp. 14, 15

[60] Gap Ruin Restoration Theories, http://www.Aig/org/articles/nab/gap-ruin-reconstruction-theories

[61] Dr. Kent Hovind and Stephen Lawwell, *The Gap Theory*, (Creation Science Evangelism, February, 2005), pp. 12, 13

[62] Discovery Health News, *"Neanderthal DNA Shows No Interbreeding With Humans"*, Nov. 15, 2006, http://health.discovery.com/news/healthscout/article.html

[63] Dr. Kent Hovind and Stephen Lawwell, *The Gap Theory*, (Creation Science Evangelism, February, 2005), p. 21

Chapter 7 – The Wonder Of It All

[64] Michael Ference, Jr., Harvey B. Lemon, and Reginald J. Stephenson, *Analytical Experimental Physics*, (T h e University of Chicago Press, 1956), p. 237

[65] Ibid., p. 234

[66] Ibid., p. 234

Chapter 8 – Living By The Law

[67] Raymond A. Serway and Jerry S. Faughn, *Holt Physics*, (Holt, Rinehart and Winston, 2002), p. 426

[68] http://en.wikipedia.org/wiki/Big_Bang

[69] Ibid

70 http://Encarta.msn.com/text_761570694_0/Big_Bang_Theory.html

71 "All About Science", http://www.big-bang-theory.com/

72 http://en.wikipedia.org/wiki/Nebular_hypothesis

73 http://www.answers.com/topic/nebular-hypothesis

74 Michael Ference, Jr., Haarvey B. Lemon, and Reginald J. Stephenson, *Analytical Experimental Physics*, (T h e University of Chicago Press, 1956), p. 98

Chapter 9 – A Commitment Of Certainty

75 The Merch Manual of Medical Information (Second Home Edition), (Merch & Company, 2003), pp. 1244, 45

Chapter 10 – Salvation Presented In Creation's Story

76 Erich Sauer, *"The Dawn Of World Redemption"*, (Wm. B. Eerdmans Publishing Company), pp. 34, 35